Cambridge Elements

Elements in the Archaeology of Europe
edited by
Manuel Fernández-Götz
University of Oxford
Bettina Arnold
University of Wisconsin–Milwaukee

INSULARITY AND IDENTITY

Prehistoric Britain and the Archaeology of Europe

Richard Bradley
University of Oxford

Shaftesbury Road, Cambridge CB2 8EA, United Kingdom

One Liberty Plaza, 20th Floor, New York, NY 10006, USA

477 Williamstown Road, Port Melbourne, VIC 3207, Australia

314–321, 3rd Floor, Plot 3, Splendor Forum, Jasola District Centre, New Delhi – 110025, India

103 Penang Road, #05–06/07, Visioncrest Commercial, Singapore 238467

Cambridge University Press is part of Cambridge University Press & Assessment, a department of the University of Cambridge.

We share the University's mission to contribute to society through the pursuit of education, learning and research at the highest international levels of excellence.

www.cambridge.org
Information on this title: www.cambridge.org/9781009557825

DOI: 10.1017/9781009557818

© Richard Bradley 2025

This publication is in copyright. Subject to statutory exception and to the provisions of relevant collective licensing agreements, no reproduction of any part may take place without the written permission of Cambridge University Press & Assessment.

When citing this work, please include a reference to the DOI 10.1017/9781009557818

First published 2025

A catalogue record for this publication is available from the British Library

ISBN 978-1-009-55782-5 Hardback
ISBN 978-1-009-55785-6 Paperback
ISSN 2632-7058 (online)
ISSN 2632-704X (print)

Cambridge University Press & Assessment has no responsibility for the persistence or accuracy of URLs for external or third-party internet websites referred to in this publication and does not guarantee that any content on such websites is, or will remain, accurate or appropriate.

For EU product safety concerns, contact us at Calle de José Abascal, 56, 1°, 28003 Madrid, Spain, or email eugpsr@cambridge.org

Insularity and Identity

Prehistoric Britain and the Archaeology of Europe

Elements in the Archaeology of Europe

DOI: 10.1017/9781009557818
First published online: April 2025

Richard Bradley
University of Oxford

Author for correspondence: Richard Bradley, richardjbradley4@gmail.com

Abstract: The Element considers historiography – the extent to which insular prehistorians have integrated their findings with the archaeology of mainland Europe; and the ways in which Continental scholars have drawn on British material. An important theme is the cultural and political relationship between this island and the mainland. The other component is an up-to-date account of prehistoric Britain and her neighbours from the Mesolithic period to the Iron Age, organised around the seaways that connected these regions. It emphasises the links between separate parts of this island and different parts of the Continent. It considers the links across the Irish Sea as only one manifestation of a wider process and treats Ireland on the same terms as other accessible regions, from France to the Low Countries. It shows how different parts of Britain were separate from one another and how they can be studied in a European framework.

Keywords: navigation, identities, coastlines, Britain, Continental Europe

© Richard Bradley 2025

ISBNs: 9781009557825 (HB), 9781009557856 (PB), 9781009557818 (OC)
ISSNs: 2632-7058 (online), 2632-704X (print)

Contents

1 'Almost the Utmost Border of the Earth'   1

2 Isolation and Inclusion (4000–2500 BC)   10

3 Far and Near (2500–1200 BC)   26

4 Questions of Time and Space (1200–54 BC)   42

5 Conclusions – The Known World   62

    References   70

1 'Almost the Utmost Border of the Earth'

Introduction

By sheer coincidence I finished work on this Element at the same time as elections took place in the United Kingdom and France. The political campaigns highlighted similar issues: national sovereignty in relation to the European Union, and the threat to national identities supposedly caused by immigration. In Britain the debate extended to devolution – should Scotland and Wales become independent states? These discussions were divisive, and most were poorly informed, but they were by no means new. Some of the same themes have influenced accounts of European prehistory. That is why this Element was written.

Archaeologists have considered similar topics and expressed similar concerns. They treated Britain as self-contained and employed it as a laboratory for investigating island archaeology. In the same way there have been studies of the European mainland which extended no further than the Channel – British archaeology is used, if at all, as a source of methods and theories. This Element reflects on those relationships, but it is primarily a review of the insular sequence in relation to broad themes in Continental prehistory. It is addressed to readers who are unfamiliar with new work in this offshore island and may not be persuaded of its relevance to European archaeology. It focuses on three subjects: the changing relationship between different parts of Britain and its neighbours; communications along and across the seaways that separate the island from the mainland; and the extent to which prehistoric Britain forms a coherent unit in scholarly research.

It is written for a series published in English and, where possible, the same applies to the sources cited in the bibliography. It is also subject to a strict word limit and for that reason the references include general syntheses or edited collections as well as individual papers. For a wider range of sources (in several languages) the reader is referred to two related publications: *The Later Prehistory of Northwest Europe* (Bradley, Haselgrove, Vander Linden & Webley 2016) and *The Prehistory of Britain and Ireland* (Bradley 2019).

Island Identities

Definitions matter. The title of this Element refers to insularity, identity, and prehistory. Why were these terms chosen, and how should they be understood?

Insularity has a double meaning. It acknowledges that Britain is an island, but it can also indicate a rejection of the wider world. During the postglacial period rising seas separated Britain from the Continent, but in the past its inhabitants either emphasised their separation or they chose to overcome it. That explains the reference to *identities*. The notion of *prehistory* refers to the time when understanding of the past depends on material remains. Written accounts are rare and problematic. Several refer to the pre-Roman Iron Age and present an outsider's view of Britain. These sources were seldom based on first-hand observation and included statements which were demonstrably wrong.

Two accounts of insular geography illustrate these points. One was written by the Greek geographer Strabo just before the Roman invasion in the first century AD. The other text was composed by the British monk Gildas 500 years later. It was composed after the imperial administration had collapsed, and the island no longer formed part of a larger European community.

According to Strabo:

> Pretannike [Britain] is in the shape of a triangle ... There are four crossings that used to go to the island from the continent ... Most of the land is flat and thickly wooded (although many places have hillocks), and it produces grain, cattle, gold, silver, and iron ... [Some of the inhabitants] who have abundant milk do not make cheese because of their inexperience, and they have no experience of gardening or other agricultural matters .... The air is rainy rather than snowy, and when it is clear it is foggy for long periods. (*Geography*: Book 4).

As an inhabitant of the island, Gildas emphasised its inaccessibility:

> Britain, situated on almost the utmost border of the earth ... stretches out from the south-west towards the north pole .... It is surrounded by the ocean, which forms winding bays, and is strongly defended by this ample and ... impassable barrier save on the south side where the narrow sea affords a passage to Gaul. It is enriched by the mouths of two noble rivers, the Thames, and the Severn (*The Ruin of Britain*: Book 2).

In their different ways Strabo and Gildas were making the same point. They epitomised a perspective that has influenced approaches to the past. In Strabo's *Geography*, the island is cut off from other parts of Europe. Its climate is harsh, and its inhabitants are unsophisticated. They share very little with people living on the European mainland. Someone raised in the Mediterranean would not have found Britain a congenial environment. Gildas takes a different line. The island has natural defences allowing its occupants to maintain their independence even after the collapse of Roman rule. Its isolation and independence constitute Brexit in reverse – the British had not withdrawn from membership of a larger Europe; instead, the Roman army had departed, and the Empire was in decline.

Some of the same assumptions influenced the work of twentieth-century prehistorians. Because Britain was located on the outer edge of Europe, they considered that its inhabitants would take a long time to become aware of developments on the Continent. The adoption of new practices, technologies, and ideas was significantly delayed. That made it difficult for archaeologists to synchronise developments on the European mainland with those on this offshore island. Before the development of radiocarbon, prehistoric chronologies depended on cross-dating. Such equations became increasingly tenuous where they extended over long distances.

These problems are illustrated by an article published long ago. One of the first researchers to study European chronology was the Swedish polymath, Montelius. By investigating the associations between distinctive artefacts in burials and hoards he was able to consider the relationship between prehistoric sequences in different countries. Absolute dates were established by links with the Mediterranean, the Aegean, and Egypt. He published a new account of Bronze Age Britain, dividing the insular sequence into five phases and proposing a fresh chronology (Montelius 1908). His findings were immediately rejected by insular scholars who preferred dates which were later than his estimates by as many as seven centuries. Today radiocarbon suggests that Montelius was largely correct. In fact, his projections were astray by just fifty to a hundred years.

A second assumption was that when significant changes did occur in Britain they followed – and in most cases were inspired by – earlier developments on the mainland. The best example of this approach is provided by a well-known monument. The building of Stonehenge was originally attributed to foreign contacts. It was assigned to the Early Bronze Age because the main setting of monoliths was compared with Mycenaean architecture. The carvings of metal axes and daggers on their surfaces were like examples in southern Europe (Atkinson 1956). The comparison is no longer credible as radiocarbon dating shows that Stonehenge was erected hundreds of years before any of its supposed prototypes.

The argument has an important corollary. Because Britain was so remote, it seemed unlikely that developments in an offshore island would have had a wider impact. Insular prehistorians were aware of Continental research, but for Childe writing his account of European prehistory in 1925 and Hawkes who published his version fifteen years later (Hawkes 1940) ideas moved in only two directions – towards the north and west. For these scholars, and for most of their contemporaries, virtually any new development in pre-Roman Britain was introduced by settlers from overseas. The preferred model was described as the 'invasion hypothesis'. The empirical basis for some of these interpretations was tenuous, and in 1966 it was reviewed in an influential article by Clark (see also Hofmann et al. 2024).

There have been several developments since then. The first was a decline in foreign language teaching in Britain. Insular prehistorians became less familiar with Continental publications. They did not read as widely as their predecessors and as a result, their own work carried less authority overseas. At the same time American 'processual archaeology' influenced scholars in Britain and Scandinavia but had a limited impact elsewhere. At its most doctrinaire it erected an intellectual barrier between British researchers and their colleagues in other parts of Europe. Proponents of the New Archaeology argued that many different processes could lead to changes in ancient society. Adaptation was at least as relevant as migration, and interpretations of the past were increasingly influenced by a kind of functionalist anthropology which has since been abandoned. Even when theoretical fashions changed and 'post-processual' archaeology took its place, the emphasis on local developments remained.

Again, the archaeology of Stonehenge is particularly informative. Where previous scholars had looked for distant parallels, Renfrew (1973) argued that the setting of monoliths was the culmination of a process of monument construction within southern England which had already extended for a thousand years. There have been revisions to his chronology, and some developments turn out to have been unexpectedly abrupt. Even so, recent accounts identify the prototypes for this extraordinary building among the timber circles already present in Britain (Gibson 2005). At the same time, they emphasise the striking contrast between insular architecture and structures of the same date on the Continent.

The notion of British separateness was illustrated by other studies. When Clark (1966) questioned the invasion hypothesis, he contrasted uncritical interpretations with two cases in which settlement from the mainland was generally accepted. One was the arrival of the first farmers during the Neolithic period, and the other was a period of colonisation by people who used Bell Beakers and metalwork. Even these interpretations have since been questioned. Perhaps domesticated resources were adopted by hunter-gatherers from their neighbours on the Continent. That was the argument of a book published by Thomas (Thomas 2013). Similarly, Burgess and Shennan (1976) were among the first to suggest that Beakers and their associations might have been associated with special practices or beliefs by the local population – these artefacts need not have expressed ethnic identities. For a while those arguments presented plausible alternatives to the established orthodoxies, and it seemed as if connections between the island and the mainland might have been overemphasised.

Recent Developments

Now the situation is changing. At a time when British separateness has become a dogma of right-wing politics, there are new ways of investigating this issue in the past. What are the best methods of documenting the movement of people and artefacts (Outram & Bogaard 2019)? And how well do traditional chronologies stand up to new methods of dating?

The study of stable isotopes preserved in human and animal bones has documented unexpected levels of mobility in the pattern of settlement; these methods show that people might have lived in more than one region during their lives. Only occasionally can the results of this research distinguish between individuals who travelled between separate parts of the island and first-generation immigrants from the Continent, but some candidates have been identified. Isotopic archaeology is limited to individual biographies, but studies of ancient DNA investigate the ancestry of whole populations (Kristiansen 2022). The results of this work have been even more dramatic and support ideas about prehistoric settlement from overseas that had become increasingly unfashionable. It is not clear how many immigrants were involved, and the same method records the genetic contribution of the indigenous population. The only caveat is that cremation burials cannot be studied by this technique.

New developments in radiocarbon dating play an equally important role. Individual determinations are more precise, and in ideal cases statistical procedures allow archaeologists to build fine-grained chronologies (Hamilton, Haselgrove & Gosden 2015; Griffiths et al. 2023). They permit more exact comparisons between British and Continental sequences. Another kind of study employs frequency distributions of radiocarbon dates to infer changing population levels and the impact of people on the environment (Shennan 2013; Woodbridge et al. 2014). Such work takes no account of conventional cultural divisions.

Conventional methods of investigating and dating the movement of people and artefacts may be reaching their limits. The classification and sequencing of artefacts do not provide such precise results as more recent approaches. Time-honoured ways of defining cultural traditions and arranging them in order are not sufficiently subtle, and in some instances, their results have even been misleading. The notion of British separateness may not stand up to scrutiny. Traditional studies have their merits, but mobility and long-distance contacts can be investigated in other ways.

If archaeological science has an important contribution to make, equally significant information comes from a different source. Over the last thirty years, the number of field projects has increased in Britain and neighbouring parts of Europe (Bradley, Haselgrove, Vander Linden & Webley 2016). Previous generations of researchers were obliged to study grave goods, hoards, and single finds because most investigations of settlements and landscapes were conducted on a small scale. That is no longer true, and more extensive projects take place in advance of commercial development. Methods vary between different parts of Europe – and even between regions of Britain – but the new information presents a challenge. The sheer extent of recent excavations permits a more thematic approach to prehistoric societies in Britain and on the Continent. It places a new emphasis on settlements, cemeteries and monuments where earlier generations were obliged to consider regional traditions through the medium of portable artefacts. This Element reflects that change of emphasis and studies of pottery and metalwork play a smaller role.

New Perspectives

How can archaeologists investigate the changing identities of Britain and its inhabitants during the prehistoric period? The present account has two starting points. One is to reconsider the relationship between different parts of this island and all its closest neighbours. Another approach is to question the idea of Britain as a geographical unit during the pre-Roman era.

Information from Ireland is commonly compared with that from Britain (Bradley 2019), but this account takes a different course. It considers Ireland, France, Belgium, north Germany, and the Low Countries, parts of which are within 500 km of the British coast (Figure 1). At times it extends even further – down the Atlantic as far as the Iberian Peninsula, and along the North Sea into South Scandinavia. But there are obvious difficulties in treating these areas on equal terms – contemporary politics carry too much weight. For instance, it has been common to treat Britain and Ireland as the 'British' Isles. This is because both islands were once ruled from London. Geographically, they are close together – the north of Ireland is visible from Scotland, and they are separated by a short sea crossing. But the same applies to the relationship between southeast England and northern France, yet their archaeological records are less often compared; important exceptions are Bourgeois & Talon (2009) and Lehoërff & Talon (2017).

Any account of the relations between Britain and its neighbours must focus on the seaways that connect them. In the past, they were contested spaces whose very names were revealing: the 'English' Channel, the 'Irish' Sea, and the North Sea which was once called the 'German' Ocean. Landing places have been identified from concentrations of prehistoric remains associated with sheltered harbours. Computer simulations have played a part and so have practical

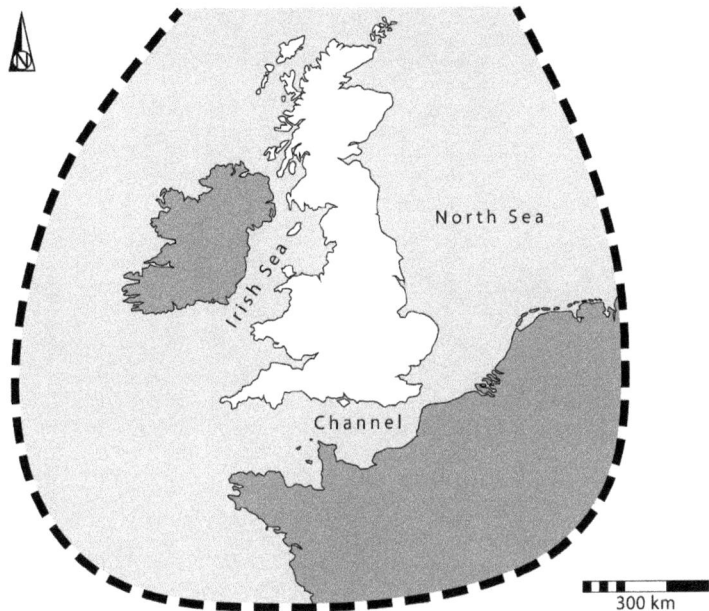

Figure 1 The island in relation to its neighbours. The shaded area shows regions within 500 km of the British coast

experiments. Among the main considerations are the visibility of landmarks and seamarks, currents, and prevailing winds (Van de Noort 2011). Although voyages were possible between France and southeast England, and between southwest Scotland and Ireland, others might have followed the shoreline until they reached the safest crossings. People travelled between different parts of Britain but need not have been aware that it was an island before it was circumnavigated by Pytheas during the fourth century BC (Cunliffe 2001a).

Lowland England was crossed by navigable rivers, but further to the north areas of high ground separated the east coast from the western seaboard. There were comparatively few ways between them (Figure 2; Fox 1932). Not surprisingly, the archaeologies of the North Sea and the Atlantic show some contrasts and for that reason each can be considered on its own terms. To some extent the same applies to the Channel. Britain was not a single entity during the prehistoric period.

The Organisation of the Text

In the light of these observations, this account is organised in two ways. Strabo described the shape of Britain as a triangle. It was bounded by seaways that met at all three of its points: Cornwall to the southwest; Kent to the southeast; and

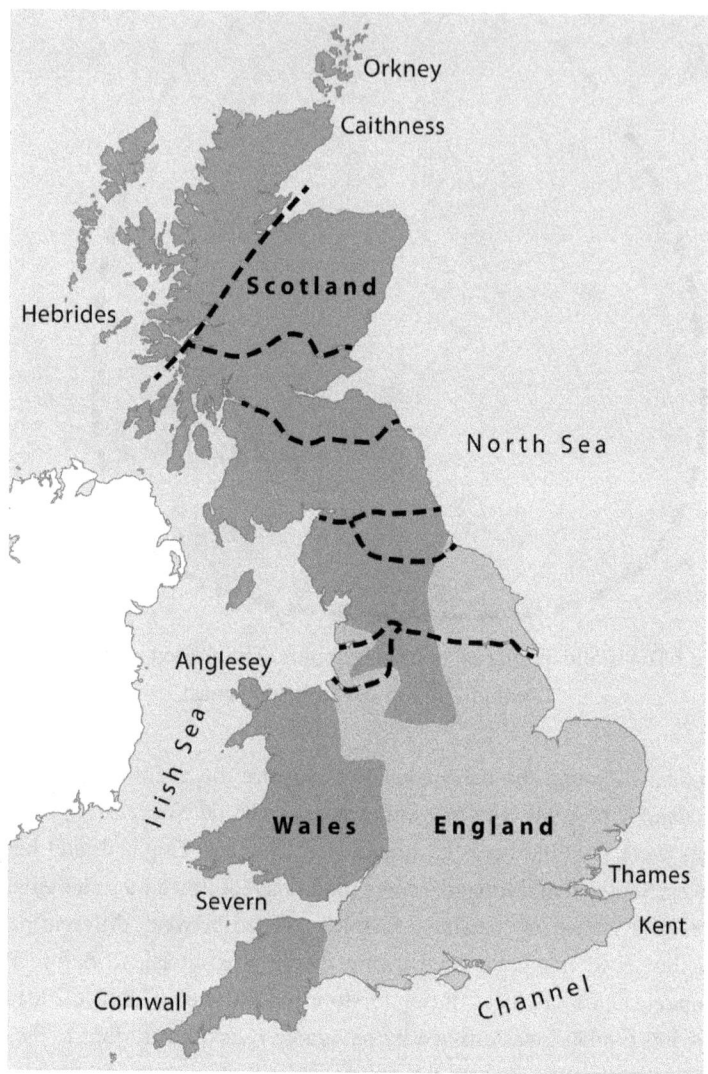

Figure 2 Prehistoric geography according to Fox (1932), emphasising upland areas and land routes between the North Sea and the Irish Sea

Caithness to the north. Beyond them there were offshore islands, the most significant of which were the Hebrides, Orkney, and Shetland. Each sea faced a different landmass, although the distances between them were not the same. The Channel linked southern England to France and Belgium (Bourgeois & Talon 2009; Lehöerff, Bourgeois, Clark & Talon 2012). The North Sea provided connections with Belgium, Germany, and the Netherlands; still further away were Denmark and Sweden (Van de Noort 2011). The narrowest divisions were across the Channel where sections of the shoreline were intervisible. The Atlantic joined Britain to Ireland and western France and, at a greater distance, to the Iberian Peninsula (Henderson 2007; Cunliffe 2010b; Moore & Armada 2011). It also connected northern Britain, Ireland, and Scandinavia. On the other hand, the sheer length of the British coast, combined with the rugged interior from northern England to the Scottish Highlands, might have meant that there were few contacts between communities living along different arms of that triangle. Lowland regions, however, were densely settled, and here journeys along rivers or overland were easier.

One starting point is to eschew the distinction prehistorians have made between the British and Continental landmasses. Instead, there will be more emphasis on the different seas that connected this island to other parts of Europe. *All Britain's neighbours will be treated on equal terms*, without privileging relationships across the Irish Sea or emphasising the special importance of the Channel; both have been common in recent scholarship. That is not to deny that some connections were more important than others, nor does it follow that close relationships existed simply because different regions could be reached from one another. Some links were thought to be important in the past, and others were rejected.

It is vital to consider each axis, contrasting developments along the North Sea with those along the Irish Sea, and comparing them with the archaeology of the Channel coast. In doing so, both sides of water must be given due weight. There were times in which communities do seem to have been closely linked. They practised a similar lifestyle. During other periods there were no such parallels, and it is important to decide whether the contrasts between them were meant to express different identities or whether they reflected phases in which there were fewer contacts.

This account falls into three sections based on absolute dates rather than technology. It begins at 4000 BC when the island of Britain was already cut off from the Continent, and the first section extends from the initial agricultural settlement to the building of extraordinary monuments like Stonehenge. By the later third millennium BC, insular ways of life were influenced by developments associated with the use of Bell Beaker ceramics and metallurgy. The second section acknowledges this development and considers the period in which new practices, new burial rites, and the movement of metals were shared across Britain and northwest Europe. It extends down to 1200 BC, by which time settlement patterns had changed in many regions. From then on, long-distance trade and conspicuous consumption played a more obvious part. There were episodes of expansion and contraction, but these developments continued largely unchecked until most of the regions considered here came into contact with the Roman Empire. Although many elements persisted afterwards, it is where this discussion will end.

2 Isolation and Inclusion (4000–2500 BC)

Again, definitions are important. In the past, isolation could be both physical and cultural, yet there was no necessary relationship between them. Britain was isolated from the mainland after sea levels rose during the postglacial period, but that did not mean the end of contacts between people in different regions. Their practices and beliefs need not have diverged significantly. Instead, the inhabitants of distant places could have emphasised their inclusion within a wider world. Both possibilities are illustrated by developments in the prehistoric period.

Other terms need equally careful handling. In this context, it is important to distinguish between *ancestry* and *descent*. Descent can be documented by the genetic evidence preserved in human bones, but ancestry is a cultural concept, governed by choice as well as parentage. Descent does not determine lifestyle, behaviour, or identity. These are choices made by living people. This distinction can be overlooked in exchanges between archaeologists and scientists (Booth 2019). There are dangers in attempting to match ancient DNA with styles of pottery. The account begins by considering when Britain became an island.

An Initial Fragmentation (10,000–4000 BC)

In 2021, an exhibition was held at the Dutch National Museum of Antiquities. It was called *Doggerland: Lost World under the North Sea* (Amkreutz & van der Vaart-Verschoof 2022). The displays covered many topics, but their starting point was the extraordinary number of artefacts recovered by dredging the seabed between the Netherlands and Britain. These finds spanned an enormous period, from the Lower Palaeolithic to the Mesolithic phase. The latest dated from the sixth millennium BC when large areas of land had already been inundated and rising water separated northern France from southern England. Even the low island represented by the Dogger Bank eventually disappeared (Figure 3). Few Neolithic items have been found in the North Sea. The exceptions are fine stone axes which might have been deposited as offerings in places which had once been significant. Whether or not one accepts this interpretation, the contrast with the Mesolithic evidence is striking.

Until the North Sea basin flooded, what is now eastern England formed part of the European continent. In 1976, Jacobi observed that before the land bridge was severed the same material culture was employed across a considerable area.

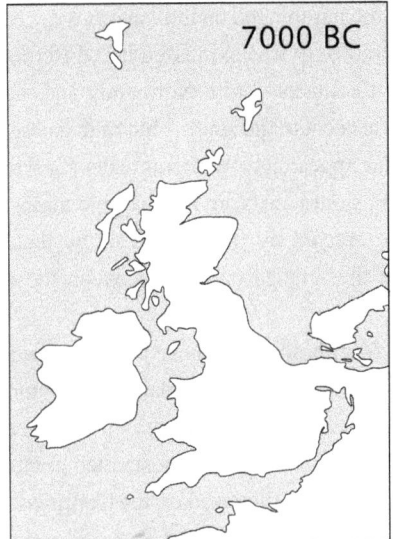 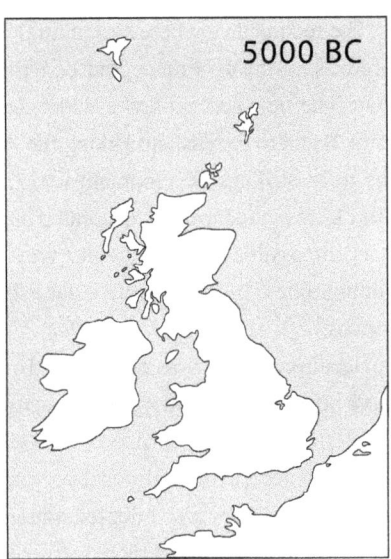

Figure 3 Britain before and after it became an island. Information from Bradley (2019)

After it happened, new kinds of artefacts were used on what was now an island. They contrasted with those in mainland Europe. His case has been supported by subsequent writers; Ballin (2016) provides a summary.

Similar developments happened on a smaller scale. To the west of Britain was Ireland, but it was separated from Scotland and Wales before it had any occupants and must have been settled by sea. That had already happened by 8000 BC. During an initial phase the inhabitants shared the same material culture as their neighbours, but this relationship had ended by 6000 BC. Otherwise, the last hunter-gatherers in Ireland became independent of their neighbours (Woodman 2015).

There were other contrasts. In two regions hunter-gatherers encountered farmers who were settling new land along the European coast. Towards the north, in the Netherlands, Germany and Denmark, both groups occupied adjacent areas and exchanged artefacts and resources for many years. Pottery was adopted by indigenous communities. It was not until 4000 BC that the new economy extended beyond the 'agricultural frontier'. The reasons for this development are uncertain, but the outcome is unambiguous (Gron & Sørensen 2018). Although wild resources were still exploited, stock raising and cereal cultivation extended into the Low Countries, north Germany, and South Scandinavia, the genetic makeup of the population changed (Allentoft et al. 2024), and people adopted a new material culture.

The second area where agricultural settlement impinged on indigenous ways of life was northwest France, but here the relationship was expressed in a different way. The new settlers had a wider range of contacts – with Normandy and the Paris Basin to the east, and along the Atlantic coast to the south – but in this case, the most striking development was the first appearance of monuments (Scarre 2011). It is evidenced by decorated standing stones, cists, and megalithic tombs. It is impossible to tell whether they were erected by immigrants or by local communities, but they were established at the time of contacts between those groups.

Because Britain was accessible by sea from both areas these developments have been used as analogies for occupation of the island (Sheridan & Pétrequin 2014). Whatever the merits of more detailed versions, several points are generally accepted. In almost every area people introduced domesticated plants and animals. They also adopted material culture like that used on the Continent. At the same time, they erected structures of the kinds built in mainland Europe. The evidence of ancient DNA provides compelling evidence of an immigrant population (Brace et al. 2019). It is obvious that British isolation was finally at an end.

Many questions remain. Was Britain entirely isolated until this phase? Did the settlement of early farmers begin in only one region, and was it restricted to a single episode of contact? Were there phases of immigration from different parts of the mainland, and how long were relations maintained with Continental communities? Such issues are difficult to resolve, but each of them touches on the relationship between insularity and identity.

Radiocarbon dates suggest that during the fifth millennium BC the native population was small (Conneller 2022). There is little to indicate long-distance contacts after Britain was cut off by sea – the only direct evidence comes from artefacts of Continental types found at a few places in southern England (Lawrence et al. 2022). Unlike the situation in Northern Europe, the last Mesolithic sites rarely contain items associated with early farmers, nor do they provide evidence of monumental architecture. Microliths are rare in the early fourth millennium BC (Griffiths 2014). Outside western Scotland (Mithen 2022) the period between about 4000 and 3500 BC marks a new beginning.

How did it happen? The evidence of ancient DNA can be interpreted in more than one way (Whittle, Pollard & Greaney 2023). So can the results of radiocarbon dating. There is no consensus, but the transition took a long while and the first developments began at different times in different regions. Taken together, they spanned almost 350 years (Whittle, Healy & Bayliss 2011, 866–71). Perhaps the people who came there used the shortest crossings between Britain and the mainland and then travelled inland from the coast.

Otherwise, the dates suggest that they followed the North Sea rather than the Channel. There may have been another axis linking northwest France to southwest England.

It is important to consider styles of material culture, and the same applies to artefact distributions, but it is just as useful to study activities which were unlikely to express local distinctiveness. One of the most significant was flint mining since a series of specialised techniques developed in France, Belgium, and the Netherlands. They were concerned with safe methods of working underground and could only have developed by trial and error. They are evidenced in southern England at the beginning of the fourth millennium BC when there were particularly close connections across the Channel (Baczkowski 2014). Ceramic technology provides another source. Again, it was learnt by experience and for that reason it can be as informative as the styles of finished vessels. A study by Pioffet (2015) identifies different ways of making pots between the east and west coasts of Britain. Her analysis is particularly important as the same procedures were followed in neighbouring parts of the Continent: northern France and southern Belgium, in one case; and Normandy and Brittany, in the other. There were more distinctive developments in northeast Scotland.

An Initial Integration (4000–3600 BC)

Although such processes extended over a significant period, their most striking feature is that they ran in parallel between Northern Europe, Britain, and Ireland (Sheridan & Pétrequin 2014; Gron & Sørensen 2018). Of course, there were local differences, but the resemblances between them outweigh any contrasts. Although these processes were associated with different styles of artefacts – in particular, axes, arrowheads, and pottery – other elements were widely shared. They included an initial emphasis on land clearance and a dispersed pattern of settlement. Cereals were represented from an early stage, but after that time there may have been greater mobility and more emphasis on livestock. Domesticated cattle, sheep, goats, and pigs were introduced to new regions. They must have been taken by boat to Britain, Ireland, and the Danish islands; the same applies to grain. Wild plants, on the other hand, remained important, and by this time hunting played a restricted role.

The surviving settlements have a limited distribution in space and time. The clearest evidence comes from Ireland where small groups of houses or isolated buildings were built in significant numbers between 3750 and 3600 BC. They have close parallels in northwest Wales but are not common in other parts of Britain (Whitehouse et al. 2014; McClatchie, Barratt & Bogaard 2016). They are equally rare on the near-Continent, although domestic dwellings are often found in South Scandinavia. In most regions they were small rectilinear structures whose plans and dimensions were like one another. The main exceptions are large timber 'halls', most of which were built in Scotland, although they resemble buildings of similar date at Mairy in northeast France (Sheridan 2013; Bradley 2021: 109–17).

Other processes were shared between the island and its neighbours. At the beginning of this period, jadeitite axes from remote sources in the Alps were brought as far as Scotland. It seems likely that their production in such spectacular settings provided the inspiration for a similar development and quarries were established in Britain and Ulster (Pétrequin et al. 2012). There is little evidence that insular products were taken across the Channel or the North Sea, but artefacts from these sources passed in both directions between England, Scotland, and Ireland. During the early fourth millennium BC there were flint mines close to the south coast; these were contemporary with similar complexes extending from Normandy to Sweden (Bostyn, Lech, Saville & Werra 2023).

Monuments

In Britain few earthworks or megalithic structures date from this early phase. Although they developed in parallel with cereal farming, the scale of monuments was not necessarily related to the intensity of land use. With this qualification, the principal developments were the building of long barrows, chambered tombs, and earthwork enclosures. Their creation raises a new problem.

The simplest way of expressing this difficulty is to contrast the histories and distributions of these structures with the material culture found in them. Why did insular monuments have so much in common with those on the Continent when the associated artefacts differ from one region to another? For example, long barrows included comparable elements on both sides of the North Sea – elongated mounds, wooden facades, and mortuary structures made from split tree trunks (Rassmann 2011) – yet each group was associated with a distinctive burial rite, and with material of kinds that conformed to local preferences.

Such patterning is not consistent with long-established approaches in which regional traditions are identified where distinctive styles of objects and monuments are found together over the same area. The method works well when it applies to ceramics and other artefacts, but in the early fourth millennium BC particular forms of stone or earthwork architecture transcended such local divisions. Special places – and the activities connected with them – made wider references.

Figure 4 The chambered tomb of Wayland's Smithy, southern England. Photograph: Creative Commons. Credit: Dickbauch

This raises another issue. Enclosures, mounds, and chambered tombs existed long before the Neolithic settlement of the island and continued to develop in different ways afterwards. They originated at a specific juncture in the archaeology of the Continent. At one time the landscape had contained substantial dwellings and whole villages, but those elements had mostly disappeared when Britain was settled. They played little part in a more dispersed pattern of settlement, yet their original importance seems to have been recalled by public architecture.

The issues are familiar from the discussion of long barrows, whose shapes and sizes have often been compared with those of longhouses (Figure 4), but it is not certain whether the histories of these structures overlapped (Whittle 2020). The resemblance between them is undeniable, but the monuments were usually a subsequent development. Either their forms recalled those of dwellings which had been occupied in the past, or they exaggerated the characteristics of the smaller buildings that eventually took their place. Recent excavations have identified the remains of rectangular dwellings overlain by Neolithic mounds or cairns. These monuments recalled the positions, rather than the plans, of ordinary houses. Most are new discoveries, and it is possible that similar traces were missed during antiquarian projects (Bradley 2023a: 37–41). A similar approach could explain the relationship between roundhouses, circular cairns and passage graves along the Atlantic, although there is not enough information on the forms of domestic buildings (Laporte & Tinévez 2005).

These arguments focus on the histories of individual dwellings, but how was monumental architecture related to *groups* of dwellings? In this case, there are signs of a more complex sequence. The settlements of longhouses in northwest Europe were sometimes bounded by ditches. During later phases, the relationship between these elements changed. At first comparable enclosures were erected close to houses that remained in occupation, or on sites where such buildings had already gone out of use. Other examples surrounded entirely open spaces and contained few features apart from pits. Enclosure ditches were usually dug in segments separated by unexcavated causeways. The sites provided a focus for the kinds of activities that had once taken place in the settlements of more sedentary communities. They included feasting, craft production, and the commemoration of the dead. It was at this stage in the sequence that such monuments were constructed in Britain, where the first of them date from the thirty-seventh century BC (Whittle 2023).

Why are these interpretations relevant to insular identities? They seem to emphasise the importance of the past. They assumed similar forms across large parts of northwest Europe. Perhaps people retained a notion of shared origins and identified themselves as part of a larger community. They drew on a notion of ancestry less precise than biological descent.

A Second Phase of Fragmentation (3600–3200 BC)

In fact such unity was more apparent than real because many of the new monuments conformed to regional groups within Britain. They may have expressed the same concerns as comparable structures on the Continent, but they also provide evidence of local alignments. For example, chambered cairns shared strong similarities between the west coast of Scotland and the north of Ireland. Long barrows, on the other hand, had comparable features to examples across the Channel and the North Sea.

Causewayed Enclosures and Cursuses

The distribution of causewayed enclosures is especially informative (Oswald, Dyer & Barber 2001). Although there were a few examples in northern Britain, the majority were constructed in regions with the closest links to the Continent – southern and eastern England. In complete contrast, a new kind of monument originated in Scotland while those earthworks were still in use. *Cursuses* were long parallel-sided enclosures that resembled avenues or roads but were closed at both ends. The oldest were constructed of wood, but later examples were defined by ditches and banks (Brophy 2016). Eventually, their distribution extended into lowland areas where it complemented that of other monuments. In some regions, cursuses avoided the positions of causewayed enclosures. The contrast is particularly obvious since their plans were so different from one

Figure 5 Map illustrating the development of causewayed enclosures and timber cursuses

another. Most enclosures were approximately circular, but cursuses followed straight alignments (Figure 5).

This development happened at a time when contacts with Continental Europe were diminishing. From this time cereal growing declined (Stevens & Fuller 2012). The population may have been lower, and areas of farmland were becoming overgrown. Slight circular buildings could have replaced rectangular houses, although the evidence is limited. Flint mines and stone axe quarries gradually went out of use and there is less evidence for the long-distance movement of artefacts. Between 3700 and 3300 BC new styles of pottery developed in Britain. These vessels were made by contrasting methods between southeast and southwest England; Welsh ceramics were different again. On the other hand, production methods suggest new links between Scotland and Ireland (Pioffet 2015). Lithic technology is less informative but suggests that contacts continued across the southern North Sea (Cleal 2012).

These changes emphasise developments along the south and east coasts of the island. One axis followed the Channel and is illustrated by the distribution of causewayed enclosures. The same applies to the main groups of flint mines which were within easy reach of the water. They were first used during the initial period of settlement but continued to function afterwards. A separate axis extended along the North Sea. In lowland England it was linked with causewayed enclosures, but further to the north it was more obviously associated with the development of cursuses. New work has identified cursus monuments in Ireland (O'Driscoll 2024), some of which shared features with those in Wales. They might provide an indication of another, western axis.

Round Mounds, Single Graves

From about 3500 BC burial mounds in Britain assumed new forms. They were associated with a new mortuary rite which was practised for about five centuries (Gibson & Bayliss 2009). Long barrows had been associated with groups of bodies, and few were provided with grave goods. There was more variety. Circular mounds and cairns had been used before, but now they became increasingly important. All these structures were associated with single inhumations accompanied by special kinds of artefacts. This tradition was first recognised a century or more ago and thanks to development-led excavations it has now been identified across most parts of Britain; between 3600 and 3300 BC there was a similar development in Ireland (Brindley & Lanting 1990). Single burials are best documented in the same areas as cursuses in England and Scotland and should date from the time when those earthworks remained in use. There is nothing to indicate links with mainland Europe.

Separation and Inclusion (3200–2500 BC)

Four developments set the course for the following centuries.

Cremation Cemeteries

After an interval of uncertain duration, the richly furnished single graves at Duggleby Howe in northeast England were covered by a mound containing deposits of cremated bone (Gibson & Bayliss 2009). This was the clearest instance of a development which also featured in the earliest phase at Stonehenge. Research has identified other cremation cemeteries in Britain (Willis 2021). While there is considerable variation, most of them date between 3100 and 2700 BC. They were associated with small circular monuments: low mounds, earthwork enclosures of various kinds, stone settings, and rings of wooden uprights. Again, many examples were near to older cursuses.

Their establishment represents a new departure in Britain, but more radical developments were happening further to the west. Relationships with Ireland became increasingly important, and so did links between Wales, northern Scotland, and lowland England. Their chronologies are not entirely clear, and each of these connections must be treated separately.

Passage Graves and Associated Monuments

Chambered Tombs

Connections with Ireland were restored after a period of isolation during the late Mesolithic period. After farming had been introduced to Britain and Ireland, the inhabitants of both islands used the same kinds of artefacts and domestic buildings. Chambered tombs played an especially important role. The evidence is strongest in the case of passage graves, which had a wide distribution among early farmers in Western Europe (Schulz Paulsson 2017). Irish examples echoed their characteristic forms but had a longer currency than their counterparts in the nearest regions of the Continent – the north and west of France. Many monuments were in cemeteries, the most elaborate of which were in the Boyne Valley not far from the Irish Sea. Here the most elaborate structures were erected between about 3200 and 2900 BC (Eogan & Cleary 2017). It seems possible that the fame of the greatest monuments – Newgrange, Knowth, and Dowth – extended beyond Ireland altogether as their architecture and a few associated objects have parallels in the Iberian Peninsula. On a smaller scale the increasing importance of cremation was shared between Britain and Ireland.

Passage graves were elaborate constructions. Bones were housed inside stone chambers concealed beneath substantial mounds or cairns but accessible from the outside world. Almost twenty per cent of the Irish examples were aligned on the midwinter or midsummer solstices. Certain sites were decorated with abstract motifs interpreted as evidence of a shared cosmology (Robin 2009). The tombs include the remains of a small number of individuals. A few of their bones had not been burnt and could be analysed for ancient DNA. A new study shows that some of the people whose remains were deposited in separate cemeteries in Ireland were distantly related to one another (Cassidy et al. 2020).

Irish tombs remained in use in the early third millennium BC and by this stage, they were addressed to larger audiences. There was a new emphasis on the spaces outside them where there were deposits of quartz, stone-lined hearths, and platforms associated with evidence of feasts (O'Kelly, Cleary & Lehane 1983). Beyond the tombs were palisaded enclosures, timber circles, and the conspicuous earthworks described as *henges* (Davis & Rassmann 2021).

Figure 6 The passage grave of Maeshowe, Orkney. Photograph: Aaron Watson

Few of those elements were shared with Continental Europe, but there were obvious links with northern and western Britain. The closest relationships were between the builders of passage graves in the Boyne Valley and the inhabitants of Orkney (Figure 6). There is no reason to suppose that new practices and beliefs were transmitted in a single direction, and it seems likely that two largely independent sequences converged during the late fourth millennium BC. Just as monument building in the Boyne Valley drew on earlier developments in Ireland, the major structures in Orkney had local antecedents.

The greatest passage tombs in Orkney, like Maeshowe and Quanterness, are compared with those in the Boyne Valley (Edmonds 2021). They were contemporary with one another, and their forms were similar. Some of them were decorated with incised motifs like those inside the large monument at Knowth. Most of the structures were associated with circular mounds. Both groups incorporated solsticial alignments, but there were differences between these buildings. The layout of the chambers resembled local house plans and contrasted with the organisation of space inside Irish tombs (Richards & Jones 2016). Orcadian monuments did not form parts of larger cemeteries. The associated burials contrasted, too. The cremation rite predominated in Ireland, but in Orkney bodies remained intact, although disarticulated bones might be rearranged: a practice that began at older long cairns.

If Irish passage graves were often grouped together, their equivalents in Orkney were separate, and some were close to settlements. Portable artefacts carried the same designs as tombs and houses. At the end of the fourth millennium BC new structures were built around large Irish monuments, although the mounds and cairns retained their importance for a long time afterwards. There was a similar development at Orcadian passage graves, which could be supplemented by an external platform or a ditch. Like Newgrange, Maeshowe might have been enclosed by a setting of monoliths (Richards 2013: 229–59). A massive walled enclosure was established nearby on the Ness of Brodgar (Card, Edmonds & Mitchell 2020). It was probably a ceremonial centre and contained a series of specialised buildings which have been compared with those identified by aerial photography close to Newgrange (Davis & Rassmann 2021).

This is not the only evidence of connections across the sea. A local style of decorated pottery – Grooved Ware – was eventually introduced to Ireland together with decorated stone artefacts (Copper, Whittle & Sheridan 2024.). Other regions played an important part. Rock art with designs related to megalithic art is represented by the west and east coasts of Britain and along the land routes leading between them (Bradley 2023b). Further links are suggested by structures around the Scottish and Irish coasts, most of which could be accessed by boat.

Henges

Earthwork enclosures indicate other connections. Although embanked 'henge monuments' have been identified close to passage graves in Ireland, most have still to be investigated and only one unusual example has any dating evidence. It was built between 2950 and 2850 BC (Cleary 2015). Such structures have been identified in the Boyne Valley and can be compared with a small number of earthworks in northern England and southwest Wales (O'Sullivan, Davis & Stout 2012).

A second group of circular earthworks suggests another axis. They have been called 'formative' henges because they predate better-known examples in Britain; their other feature is that they have internal banks and external ditches. Their distribution extends from northwest Wales to Wessex (Burrow 2010a). Little is known about them, but those with radiocarbon dates were first built by 3000 BC. They include two excavated monuments. At Bryn Celli Ddu on the island of Anglesey one of these enclosures contained a small passage grave and a stone circle associated with cremation burials (Burrow 2010b). The tomb was enlarged around 3000–2900 BC and resembles structures of the same age in Ireland (Figure 7). A second example was Stonehenge where a circular enclosure with a segmented ditch was built at about the same time. It seems to have contained another ring of standing stones which were introduced from southwest Wales. The new structure was associated with cremation burials like those

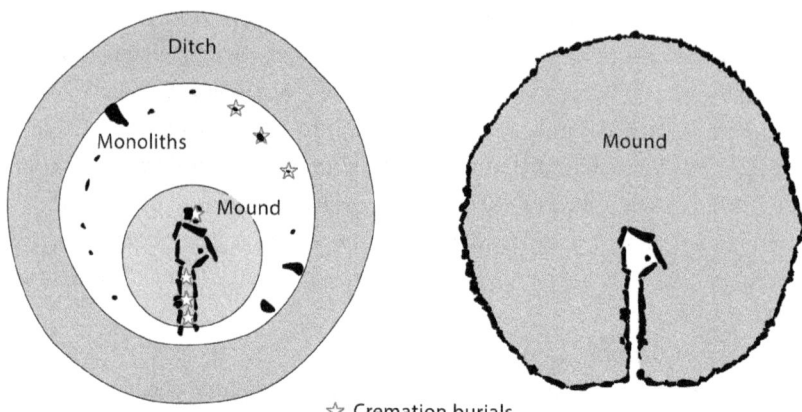

Figure 7 The sequence at Bryn Celli Ddu, Anglesey, showing the positions of the cremation burials.

at Bryn Celli Ddu – links between western Britain and other regions were not confined to the Irish Sea. In this case, they were emphasised by the transport of building material (or a dismantled monument) over 200 km (Parker Pearson et al. 2020).

Later Connections

After an initial phase, elements that had originated in Orkney were adopted in other parts of Britain. They were associated with the same ceramic tradition – Grooved Ware – but assumed different forms. Towards the east coast there is less evidence of monumental architecture (apart from a group of henges with two concentric earthworks which have not been dated). There were mines and other sources of high-quality flint close to the water and artefacts made there were distributed along the North Sea from southeast England to northeast Scotland (Gardiner 2008).

The most conspicuous monuments were henges with one internal ditch and an external bank (Figure 8). There were also large palisaded enclosures, some of which were erected in the same places. For the most part they were established in regions with cremation cemeteries and major cursuses. There were important contacts along both the Atlantic and the North Sea. Connections with northern Scotland are illustrated by rock art which included unusual motifs associated with Orkney chambered tombs. Some of the decorated outcrops were by sheltered inlets while others followed land routes leading through the high ground (Bradley 2023b).

The largest monuments could have been visited from distant regions, and the structures found inside them – especially the stone or timber circles – had

Figure 8 Henge monument enclosing a stone circle at Arbor Low, northern England. Photograph: Creative Commons. Credit: Thebrainchamber 1

similar plans across Britain and Ireland. A few resembled one another so closely that they might have been intended as copies; the distances between such pairs were between 250 and 400 km (Bradley 2024). Certain henges provide evidence of feasts. Isotopic analysis shows that animals were brought over considerable distances (Madgwick et al. 2019). Large work forces were needed to build these structures, and numerous people must have taken part in ceremonies. Most of the biggest henges and palisaded enclosures were in the west and south of Britain, but timber circles are also found towards the east. Fewer of them were enclosed and they might have had different histories from the others.

The erection of important monuments made great demands, and it is not always clear where suitable material was found. The transport of monoliths to Stonehenge was not a unique instance. Other settings combined rock from several sources, and examples from Orkney to southwest England suggest that individual monuments combined the efforts of several communities and might have been designed as microcosms of a wider landscape. At times these connections are especially revealing. Stonehenge itself employed building material obtained close to a great monument of the same date at Avebury (Nash et al. 2020).

Avebury was within sight of the greatest artificial mound in prehistoric Europe. It introduces yet another issue. Silbury Hill was one of a small group of earthworks in central southern England, although there are possible parallels in north Wales and southwest Scotland (Leary, Field & Campbell 2013). It was constructed between 2500 and 2400 BC, at a time when Newgrange remained significant (Carlin 2017), but unlike that famous monument Silbury was not associated with any burials.

Figure 9 Stonehenge: Photograph: Aaron Watson

The Implications of Stonehenge

The principal monument at Stonehenge is dated between 2580 and 2475 BC (Figure 9). How is it relevant to identities in prehistoric Britain? Following a prescient suggestion of Childe, Parker Pearson argues that at different times it celebrated the unification of regional traditions within Britain (Parker Pearson 2023: 158–60; Parker Pearson et al. 2024). The process started with the introduction of bluestones from Wales, and in a later phase it brought together building materials from other sources. It combined structural elements that had developed in timber buildings throughout Britain and Ireland and made unique demands on human labour, organisation, and skills (Gibson 2005). It united disparate elements in one unprecedented project. It seems possible that other monuments played comparable roles but on more local scales, and it is no accident that most of them were located in between two separate networks. One followed the North Sea, and the other connected Wales and western Scotland to Ireland. Although there were close links across the Irish Sea, Britain was isolated from the Continent.

Discussion

The opening section of this Element asked how the archaeology of prehistoric Britain was related to that of other parts of Europe. The Mesolithic and Neolithic periods show how difficult it is to provide any simple answers. There were significant changes in the shape of the land and the contacts between people who occupied different regions. There were connections that the inhabitants chose to foster and those they decided to neglect. Few of the new alignments correspond to national boundaries today and in a period when travel by sea was important the distinction between islands and the mainland was not necessarily significant. During the Neolithic period the inhabitants were free to ally themselves with other communities or to keep their distance. Thus, Britain had few contacts with Ireland between 6000 and 3800 BC, and then the two islands had close links until the late fourth millennium. At that stage, they became caught up in a series of dramatic developments that had nothing in common with events in mainland Europe.

If people could decide between promoting or rejecting long-distance contacts, their decisions were influenced by several factors. One was the ease or difficulty of travelling between Britain, Ireland and the Continent. At an early stage there was an obvious emphasis on the securest routes. By the Late Neolithic, however, more arduous journeys were undertaken, especially those around the north of Scotland where a series of monument complexes developed in remote locations. Going there involved a challenging passage by sea. This must have been one of the reasons why these places became so important. It is vital to recognise the entire range of possibilities. People and their livestock crossed the water where it was safest to do so, but visitors to special locations – quite possibly pilgrims – might have invited difficulties as a way of asserting their beliefs (Bradley & Watson 2024).

Other connections involved the forms of monuments rather than the locations in which they were built. The appearance of long mounds and causewayed enclosures evoked structures occupied long before farmers settled in Britain. In the same way, passage graves were still erected in the north and west of the island after they had gone out of use in the nearest parts of the Continent – they may have had a similar significance. Other kinds of connections formed during the late fourth and early third millennia BC when the layout of impressive monuments acknowledged the positions of the sun at the turning points of the year. Ideas about the working of the cosmos united the occupants of different regions, even if they rarely met.

Which networks were most important, and did they extend beyond this offshore island? Do they lend any support to the idea of British self-sufficiency? In fact, there were several changes of alignment during the Neolithic period. After the social and physical disruption caused by sea level rise there were remarkably close links between the island, its neighbour to the west, and the European mainland. That is generally accepted, but it is harder to explain why they weakened over time. Nor is it clear why more local networks developed. One was associated with the invention of a specifically insular kind of monument.

Cursuses were most clearly evidenced along the North Sea coast from Scotland to Wessex. Their adoption in southern England seems to have disrupted the connections with the Continent epitomised by causewayed enclosures. Another axis was developing in the west. It is most clearly evidenced by megalithic tombs. Its origins lay in links with Atlantic Europe and more immediately with Ireland. In Britain, there was a noticeable contrast between these zones.

That was especially true in the north where communications between the east and west coasts were difficult because of the high ground in between them. But other alignments are equally revealing. There were fewer regional distinctions within lowland England where it was comparatively easy to travel along the river system. In the far north the sea played a greater role, and in the centuries around 3000 BC Orkney had closer links with Ireland than with parts of mainland Scotland. At a time when relations with the Continent had lost their attraction, there was more interchange across the Irish Sea. During the Neolithic sequence British communities seem to have switched their attention from one neighbour to another. Instead of initial connections with France, Belgium, and the Low Countries there was a stronger relationship with Ireland.

In the end events took an unexpected turn. In many parts of Britain enormous monuments were erected during the mid third millennium BC. They conformed to local types but seem to have been the outcome of the same stimulus. Their construction might have promoted a new unity, but this development was provoked by developments outside the island altogether. The settlement of new people from the Continent changed the nature of insular prehistory.

3 Far and Near (2500–1200 BC)

2500–2200 BC

Bell Beakers

Discussions of long-distance contacts are complicated by questions of terminology. During the third millennium BC similar styles of pottery were important in two parts of the Continent. In Northern Europe there was *Corded Ware* and further to the west there were *Bell Beakers* (Vander Linden 2024). The relationship between them is not clearly understood. Where did they originate? Were they employed in sequence, or were they used at the same times but in different regions?

In Britain these questions are seldom asked because Corded Ware is absent, and the Bell Beaker tradition was introduced from the mainland. But these pots and their associations raise a special problem. How were they related to

Continental styles and what light does their adoption shed on relations between this island and other parts of Europe (Figure 10)? The difficulties are illustrated by a scheme devised by Clarke (1970).

His classification of these vessels mixed three different elements. First, he described their decoration. There were *All-over Corded Beakers* and *Barbed Wire Beakers*. A second group comprised styles shared between different parts of Britain and regions of the Continent: as well as *European Bell Beakers*, there were *Wessex / Middle Rhine Beakers*, *Northern / Middle Rhine Beakers*, and *Northern / Northern Rhine Beakers*. He defined another tradition which he termed *Primary Northern British / Dutch*. He argued that all these styles were

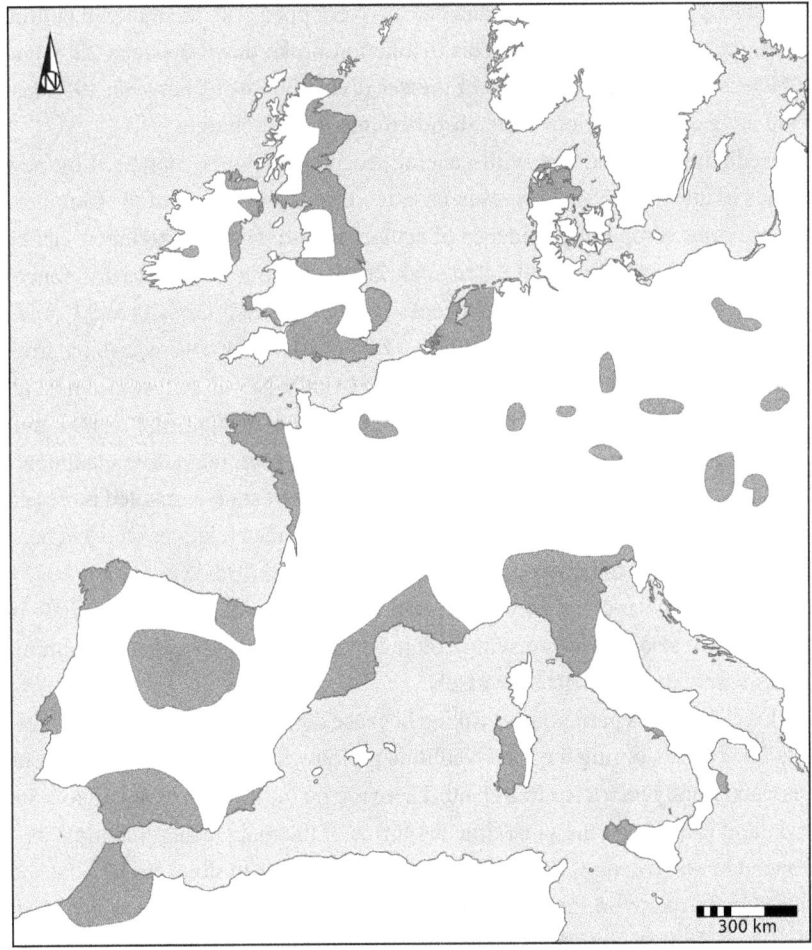

Figure 10 The distribution of Bell Beaker pottery. Information from Vander Linden (2024)

associated with groups of immigrants who introduced new burial rites and the earliest metalwork. He also identified local sequences in Southern and Northern Britain, respectively. Another regional type was the *East Anglian Beaker*.

His classification was too complex, and from the outset some of its elements were questioned by Continental scholars. As a result, simpler chronologies were proposed, first by Case (1993) and then by Needham (2005). Their interpretations are supported by radiocarbon dating. Needham followed previous writers in accepting an initial phase of settlement from the mainland. Like Case, he recognised the importance of contacts across the Channel and the southern North Sea, as well as other links extending along the Atlantic. He identified three successive developments in Britain. Between 2500 and about 2300 BC Bell Beakers and their associations were like those in mainland Europe. They indicated a period of migration and hardly overlapped with the material culture of the indigenous inhabitants. This distinction broke down between 2300 and 1950 BC, when there were signs of greater diversity. Lastly, between 1950 and 1700 BC, Beaker traditions were absorbed into insular culture.

Needham's scheme met with general acceptance and is supported by new studies of ancient DNA. This research extends to most regions of the Continent and provides compelling evidence of settlers whose genetic inheritance can be traced to southeast Europe (Olalde et al. 2018). Despite important differences between their mortuary rites, the people buried with Bell Beakers and Corded Ware shared ancestors in the steppes. The British results were distinct from those obtained for local burials of Early and Middle Neolithic dates (almost all Late Neolithic burials were cremations). Still more striking, the genetic evidence did not document a significant contribution from the native inhabitants for about 500 years. Of course, this method could not study cremated bone and the inhumations associated with Beaker pottery included relatives who had been buried together in the same cemeteries (Booth, Brück, Brace & Barnes 2021). But the new scheme agrees with Needham's interpretation of the artefacts in graves. It is also consistent with isotopic evidence of first-generation immigrants associated with Beaker vessels.

This evidence is particularly striking because communities in Britain had few outside contacts during the Late Neolithic period when their wider connections were apparently restricted to Ireland. There are no indications of any links with mainland Europe. At the same time the forms of the main insular monuments – from cursuses to henges and from palisaded enclosures to stone circles – lacked close counterparts on the European mainland. A possible exception is a great timber circle at Pömmelte in central Germany (Spazier & Bertemes 2018), but even its form may have been inspired by the remains of the Continental earthworks known as *roundels* which had been used at an earlier date (Schier

2023). The insular henges and stone circles had originated by 3000 BC, but the first examples were mainly in northern and western Britain. Later monuments show a remarkable contrast. They were more elaborate and building them required bigger labour forces. The same elements were shared across larger areas. Radiocarbon dating suggests that they were erected over a short period during the mid to late third millennium BC. They were associated with a local ceramic style, Grooved Ware.

There was a dramatic escalation in the scale of special buildings. Their dates suggest that they were constructed at a time when people were becoming aware of new practices on the Continent. They would also have encountered groups of immigrants within Britain itself. Certain monuments were unusually short-lived. Others were erected after the first settlers had arrived. The simplest interpretation is that this emphasis on new projects was a reaction to the influence of unfamiliar people and strange beliefs – it reasserted insular traditions on an unprecedented scale (Greaney et al. 2020). Although there are few indications of violent conflicts, local identities were threatened, and British separateness was gradually undermined.

New Networks

This was the second major phase of immigration from the Continent, but it followed a different course from the settlement of the first farmers a millennium and a half before. The Bell Beaker occupation of Britain appears to have been more rapid and covered a greater area. A new study shows that the burials of the first immigrants were widely distributed (Parker Pearson et al. 2019). If the best-known example is the Amesbury Archer whose grave was in Wessex (Fitzpatrick 2011), another was on a Hebridean island. A striking number of Beaker sites were by the sea. Some of those locations had been utilised as landing places and harbours during earlier periods, but the use of others was new (Bradley, Rogers, Sturt & Watson 2016).

The sources of these settlers were as diverse as those of the Early Neolithic phase. The separate styles defined by Clarke placed an emphasis on the Netherlands and the Rhineland. He also distinguished between artefact assemblages in northern Britain and those found further to the south: a contrast echoed in Needham's subsequent analysis. Case stressed the importance of a second network extending up the west coast of Europe from Iberia. This network impinged on southern England. In the Late Neolithic phase there is evidence of travel around the British and Irish coasts, but the new connections were not the same. Contacts along the North Sea and the Channel increased in importance, and the close links between Orkney and the Boyne Valley lapsed. Of greater significance were those between Britain and the Continent. They allied the offshore island with areas as far from one another as the Netherlands and Brittany. Although relations with Ireland had been important, there could not be a greater contrast with the insularity of Britain during the previous phase.

Houses and Burials

At the same time, there were regional contrasts during the Beaker period. The distributions of portable artefacts have played a prominent part in the discussion, but other features are more revealing. The main sources of information are the forms of settlements and houses, and the treatment of the dead.

A recent publication discussed Bell Beaker houses in different parts of Europe (Gibson 2019). One feature shared between Britain, Ireland and the near-Continent is the rarity of recognisable dwellings. Most occupation sites are marked by scatters of artefacts, and features such as post holes, hearths, and pits are comparatively uncommon. Domestic buildings have been identified in Denmark and Brittany but are unusual in other places; they are equally infrequent in Ireland. For the most part their forms were like those of older structures in the same regions, and this applied to the few circular or oval examples in Britain. In western Scotland, however, a new type has been recognised. It was approximately boat-shaped. Few have been excavated, but they compare with houses of the same kind in Brittany and Normandy. The evidence from other parts of the Continent shows a fundamental contrast. Although domestic buildings are uncommon in the Netherlands – one of the regions with the strongest connections to Britain – the excavated structures were really longhouses. They are so rare that they may have played an exceptional role. Although the evidence for domestic buildings is limited, there was no single type of Beaker house in Europe.

Burial rites did not conform to the same regional distinctions. Individual inhumations, associated with pottery, ornaments, and metalwork were widely distributed. They took similar forms throughout Britain and the nearest parts of the Continent but were unusual in Ireland. The most complex burials were placed inside wooden chambers or coffins and some of them were associated with circular mounds or enclosures; others were in flat graves which could form parts of larger cemeteries (Figure 11; Vander Linden 2024). Single burials were a new development in Britain where their only equivalents had gone out of use 500 years before (Brück 2019: 16–50). On the other hand, groups of round mounds in the Netherlands were already associated with Corded Ware. Some of these earthworks were reused during the Bell Beaker period, and more were constructed at that time (Bourgeois 2013).

Figure 11 Early Bronze Age barrows on the Wessex chalk. Photograph: Creative Commons. Credit: Jim Champion

A different tradition is recorded along the Atlantic coast. In western France, there were collective burials as well as the single graves that characterised other regions. Many of these deposits were associated with the remains of older monuments. Chambered tombs saw a second period of use. Their chronology is revealing since there seems to have been a preference for older monuments rather than those erected during the recent past (Gibson 2016). The evidence reinforces the distinction between one network based on the Channel and the southern North Sea, and another along the Atlantic. There was little overlap between the axes indicated by graves, and those defined by domestic dwellings.

Copper

It is often supposed that the settlement of people from the Continent is explained by the search for metals, but the earliest evidence for the extraction of copper comes from southwest Ireland around 2400 BC and predates the establishment of similar mines in Britain by 300 or 400 years. The Irish site was at Ross Island where the mines were associated with a work camp in which the ore was processed (O'Brien 2004). It was associated with Beaker pottery and with a distinctive technology practiced in parts of Atlantic Europe.

The adoption of metalwork provides further evidence of connections between Britain and its neighbours. Copper was taken across the Irish Sea, but certain artefacts shared a distinctive composition defined as 'Bell Beaker metalwork' (Needham 2012). It could have combined material from several sources. That raises a problem, but its distribution suggests links between Britain, Holland, and Normandy. It provides a further indication of the affinities between insular communities and those in accessible regions of the Continent.

2200–1600 BC

Metals remained important during this phase. At one time the distribution of the earliest goldwork suggested a source in Ireland, but newer research favours an origin in southwest England (Standish, Dhuime, Hawkesworth & Pike 2015). That connection is revealing as the same area became a major source of tin from 2200 BC. It was alloyed with copper and widely distributed in Western Europe. This marks the beginning of the insular 'Bronze Age'. Far from emphasising British isolation, it was a precocious development and anticipated technological changes in neighbouring regions by 200–300 years (Pare 2000). About 1900 BC the copper mines at Ross Island had been replaced by the first examples in Wales and northern England; others were established in Ireland from 1800 BC (Timberlake 2016). They operated on a smaller scale and insular communities became increasingly dependent on supplies from the Continent.

The same kinds of artefacts were associated with harbours and landing places on the coast. Most of these sites had been used before (Bradley, Rogers, Sturt & Watson 2016). Such locations were set apart from settlements and monuments of the same date and could have been where strangers met to exchange artefacts. The distribution of these places is limited to areas in which the ancient shoreline survives but 'maritime havens' of this kind are recorded along the North Sea and both shores of the Irish Sea.

The Power of the Past

One reason why scholars had been reluctant to countenance episodes of migration from the Continent was the frequency with which Beaker and Early Bronze Age artefacts were discovered at Neolithic sites. The greatest concentrations of burials focused on stone or earthwork structures surviving from the past. The area around Stonehenge provides the obvious example of this relationship (Booth, Brück, Brace & Barnes 2021). The contents of local graves have been studied for ancient DNA. Laboratory analysis showed that the people buried there were not related to the original builders of the monument. They might have owed their authority to an invented past. Radiocarbon dating of individual grave goods together with human and animal bones reinforces this impression, for it shows that some of the deposits contained heirlooms or relics which had been taken from other contexts. The artefacts could be worn or broken and some of the necklaces accompanying the deceased combined beads from different sources (Woodward & Hunter 2015). This concern with a remote past was not confined to Britain, and the same model explains why Breton megalithic tombs were reused during the Beaker period (Gibson 2016).

At the same time, those developments focused on certain regions of Britain at the expense of others. It is often supposed that older styles of monuments lapsed by the Early Bronze Age and that new ones were no longer built. That was largely true in lowland England, but henges and stone circles were still constructed in other areas. They resembled their predecessors but were conceived on a smaller scale. It seems as if established practices and beliefs retained their power in the north and west after their abandonment in the south (Bradley & Nimura 2016).

Settlements, Houses, and Landscapes

The archaeology of this period in Britain is dominated by burial mounds, and it has been surprisingly difficult to investigate the settlement pattern (Brück 2019; Johnston 2021). The same problem affects research in other parts of Europe, especially Ireland, France, and the Low Countries. There is no shortage of living sites, but in most cases all that survive are collections of artefacts. A common response has been to infer a mobile pattern of settlement in which the raising of domesticated animals was more important than cultivation. Finds of cereals are uncommon although they do occur, but the argument is largely circumstantial. Stable isotopes provide a more reliable source of information. On the Continent this kind of study has been undertaken for two main reasons – to investigate prehistoric migrations and the exchange of individuals between communities (Stockhammer & Massy 2022). In Britain it sheds more light on mobile land use. A new analysis of burials dating from the late third and early second millennia BC showed that people could have lived in several regions over the course of their lives (Parker Pearson et al. 2019). At the same time, they might be buried outside those areas. What led to that decision? Perhaps it was determined by the continuing influence of the past, as some of the most elaborately furnished graves were associated with monuments built during the Neolithic period.

Domestic buildings are uncommon in Britain, but the examples identified in lowland regions are roundhouses which are smaller and slighter than those occupied during later phases. With occasional exceptions, they are associated with few artefacts and might not have been inhabited for long periods (Brück 2019: 118–21). By contrast, more robust constructions have been recognised in the north where their remains survive on marginal land. They are more like the dwellings occupied during subsequent phases (Pope 2015). They seem to be associated with irregular walled plots and clearance cairns and are attributed to a phase of upland settlement that took advantage of the favourable climate at this time. The same argument explains the large number of specialised monuments – round barrows and stone circles – found in the vicinity, but any direct relationship between these features has been difficult to substantiate.

Another way of viewing the evidence from highland Britain is to suggest that land was exploited seasonally. It would have been a sensible strategy, as it could prevent – or at least slow down – the deterioration of the local soils and the creation of poorly drained moorland. There is a direct comparison with another development during this phase. It was when large areas in southern England were cleared and turned into heathlands. Until recently, the distribution of heathland soils was treated as evidence for a short-lived phase of colonisation from more stable environments: an ill-judged attempt at economic extensification that failed (Bradley 2019: 202). It was never clear why the newly opened land contained few occupation sites. New research in South Scandinavia suggests an explanation (Haughton & Løvschal 2023). Provided it was managed by regular burning, heathland could provide extensive and valuable grazing. Far from being impoverished – a refuge for people excluded from more productive areas – it provided a vital resource, shared by different communities engaged in the management of livestock. That development was not restricted to Jutland where it has been studied in most detail. It extended to the Low Countries at exactly the time when their inhabitants were in contact with lowland Britain. Although the history of heathland grazing on the Continent goes back to the Corded Ware phase, it continued, and may even have expanded, during this phase. Perhaps similar practices were adopted on both sides of the North Sea.

On the other hand, differences of domestic architecture remained important. While roundhouses were occupied in Britain and Ireland, the inhabitants of the Low Countries preferred to live in longhouses. A small number have been identified in parts of northeast Europe where their forms anticipate those of later dwellings. They also occur in northeast and northwest France, although there is evidence of oval or circular structures in Normandy (Bradley, Haselgrove, Vander Linden & Webley 2016: 155–7). Domestic dwellings were very different in east Central Europe where the settlements of the Únětice Culture included enormous rectangular buildings whose proportions compare with those of Neolithic structures (Risch, Friederich, Küssner & Meller 2022). The contrast is particularly striking since Únětice burials share elements with graves in Wessex.

Long-Distance Links

New networks linked the principal concentrations of monuments. They can be identified on several scales. There were striking similarities across the Channel and the Irish Sea. Concentrations of round barrows are found on both sides of the water: in Kent in southeast England, and in Flanders and the Somme on the opposite shore (Bradley, Haselgrove, Vander Linden & Webley 2016: 126–31). Similarly, cist cemeteries featured along the east coast of Ireland, and in the west of Scotland where they included artefacts with Irish parallels.

Another series of graves shared features between both sides of the Channel: from Cornwall to Kent in southern England, and from Brittany to the Rhine on the mainland. In this case the connecting link was the presence of vessels made of gold, amber, and shale. They were finely crafted and might have been used on special occasions (Needham, Parfitt & Varndell 2006). These connections extended from northwest France to the Netherlands. For the most part they were between regions that faced one another across the water. It is easy to treat them as separate 'territories', but this does not do justice to the similarities between their material culture, and the extent of contacts by sea. They must have possessed a special character. Needham (2009) has introduced the useful term 'maritory' to describe the links between them.

Other networks extended further still. Within Britain they linked gold ornaments used as grave goods in Wessex with similar material buried in Orkney. There were connections between richly furnished burials in southern England and their equivalents in Brittany (Needham 2000). Other links formed with the Únětice Culture where a few outstanding deposits contained artefacts that originated in Britain (O'Connor 2010). Vandkilde (2017) envisages close links between the sources of Baltic amber in South Scandinavia and two regions where it was deposited in graves – Wessex and east Central Europe (it is also represented by a few finds in Brittany). The best-known relationship linked these regions to the Aegean. Amber beads were made in England before they were exported and buried at Mycenae. There seem to have been other connections, but such patterns were exceptional.

There is even more evidence for long-distance contacts. Kristiansen and Larsson (2005) recognise two main zones of interaction during the earlier second millennium BC (Figure 12). They describe one of them as the 'western steppe corridor'. It linked Anatolia, the Carpathians, and east Central Europe to South Scandinavia. The other was a 'Mediterranean corridor' that linked Britain, Ireland and northwest France to northern Italy, and the Mediterranean from Sicily to the Aegean and Crete. Both spheres overlapped, and the more westerly network extended for almost

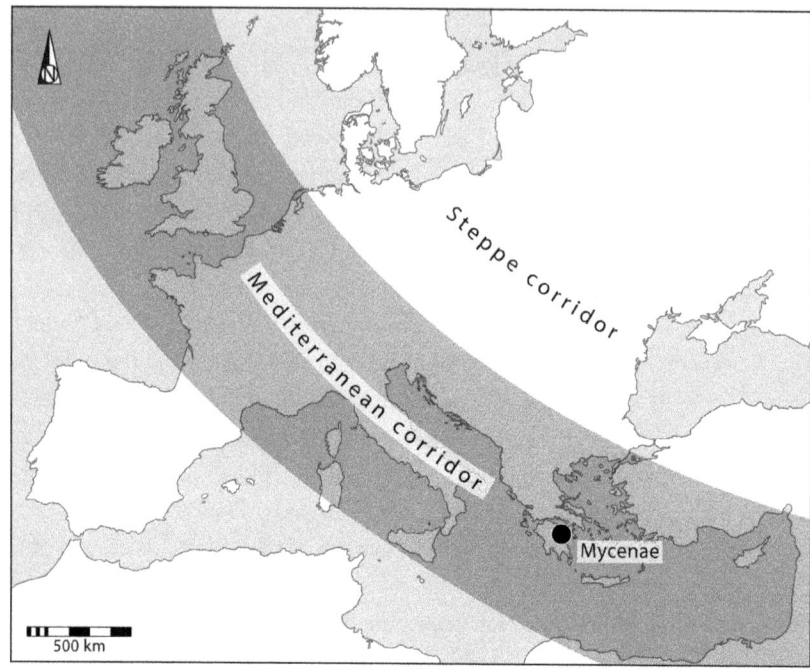

Figure 12 Major zones of contact in Early Bronze Age Europe

4,000 km. Britain was at one end of a long chain of connections, but it occupied a place in a wider world.

1600–1200 BC

Crisis and Denouement?

In a paper published in 2015, Risch and Meller drew attention to changes in the archaeological record around 1600 BC. Their discussion was in two parts. The first concerned events in the Mediterranean and the aftermath of the eruption of Santorini. They joined a wider discussion of the collapse of Minoan society on Crete and Mycenaean developments in Greece. Then they turned to important changes in regions that have featured here: Britain, Brittany, the Low Countries, South Scandinavia, and east Central Europe. Did they share the same cause? It seemed unlikely that a disaster in the Mediterranean would have had such lasting effects on the climate that it affected settlement in remote areas. Yet societies in distant parts of Europe participated in long-distance networks that extended to the Aegean, and those connections might have been put at risk. For Risch and Meller such links were concerned with ideology and cosmology rather than everyday affairs, and an inexplicable disaster might have undermined people's confidence in long-established beliefs.

Such a crisis would not have had far-reaching effects unless local systems were already under strain, and the scheme proposed by Risch and Meller needs to be combined with information from other areas. Two features are widely documented. The first is a predilection for finely crafted grave goods, and for items obtained from (or shared with) distant areas. That is how connections with Southern Europe first became important and why events in the Mediterranean could have had wider consequences. Another problem was more local. By this phase the organisation of barrow cemeteries in Britain and on the near-Continent had become exceptionally complex. There were many separate mounds. Some had been rebuilt, and others were added to existing groups. The monuments could be organised according to increasingly complex spatial patterns. Radiocarbon dating shows that the construction of barrows in the Low Countries peaked between 1700 and 1500 BC, and then it ceased (Bourgeois 2013). It also ended in Brittany around 1500 BC (Needham 2000). Similarly, linear cemeteries in southern England were established towards 1600 BC and were not built after that time (Garwood 2007). Like their counterparts across the North Sea, they might have recorded the relationships between the dead buried beneath separate mounds.

These developments added one more layer of significance to funerary landscapes which were already full of meanings. Perhaps the process was approaching its limits. These distinctions were becoming too complex to develop much further. Large barrow cemeteries like those in Wessex, northern France or the Low Countries no longer offered the ideal medium for displaying social distinctions. In the same way, an elaborate building like Stonehenge which had been constructed and elaborated over many years provided too much information to communicate its message effectively. After 1600 BC it seems to have been abandoned (Cleal et al. 1995). If events in the Mediterranean resulted in a loss of confidence on a European scale, local sequences might have become unstable for other reasons.

In Britain it is difficult to date the decline in barrow building exactly, and small funerary monuments remained important for some time; there were also flat cemeteries in which many of the burials were in urns (Cooper 2016). Similar deposits are recorded as secondary deposits in and around older mounds. Risch and Meller describe this development as a social 'collapse' but it is hard to accept their conclusion when the consumption of bronze weapons actually increased – their contexts simply changed from graves to rivers (Bradley 2017: 152–4). These authors could not have foretold a more basic objection to their interpretation. When they wrote their article in 2015, it was accepted that most metal had been introduced to Britain from the Continent and that the mines in Wales and northern England operated on a limited scale; the same applied to their counterparts in Ireland. One of the insular sources was Great Orme in northwest Wales where extraction started around 1700 BC. A new study shows that production increased considerably from 1600 BC and remained at a high level for two centuries. Output was far greater than originally believed and a new analysis shows that Great Orme provided much of the copper consumed in Britain, although it was not the only source of supply (Williams 2023; Needham & Wilkin 2024). It was also exported to Continental Europe where the distribution of its products reached from western France to Sweden. The expected relationship between the offshore island and its neighbours was reversed.

Settlements, Landscapes, and Houses

In his recent publication Williams (2023) considers the distribution of metal from Great Orme and suggests the routes along which it was transported. It was taken around the coast by sea and across the water to Ireland, northern France, the Rhineland, the Netherlands, and South Scandinavia. It was exported from beaches close to the mines, and from southern Wessex and the Thames estuary. Copper was also carried along long-distance paths within Britain and by the river network. This required a suitable infrastructure, and these developments were made possible by the availability of plank-built boats, the construction of wooden trackways and bridges, and by the existence of increasingly open conditions.

New developments seem to have been underway from 1600 BC and possibly earlier (Brück 2019; Johnston 2021). Their most striking features have been recognised in lowland England. Among them were substantial roundhouses, ditched or fenced enclosures, small cremation cemeteries, and agricultural facilities including storage pits, granaries, droveways, wells, and ponds (Bradley 2019: 218–27). Cereals were cultivated on an increasing scale, but one of the most obvious features was the creation of field systems defined by banks, ditches, hedges, or rows of posts (Figure 13). Some conformed to a rectilinear layout and extended across large areas (Yates 2007). They could be organised around solsticial alignments (Gosden et al. 2021: 248–51) – this was one concern that had been inherited from the past (Needham 2024). Another was the way in which these field boundaries incorporated the positions of older barrows.

New research suggests additional details. The earliest evidence of regular land divisions is found near the English coast and must have been contemporary with the main barrow cemeteries further inland. From about 1500 BC more field systems developed in the regions closest to the Continent. By that time large

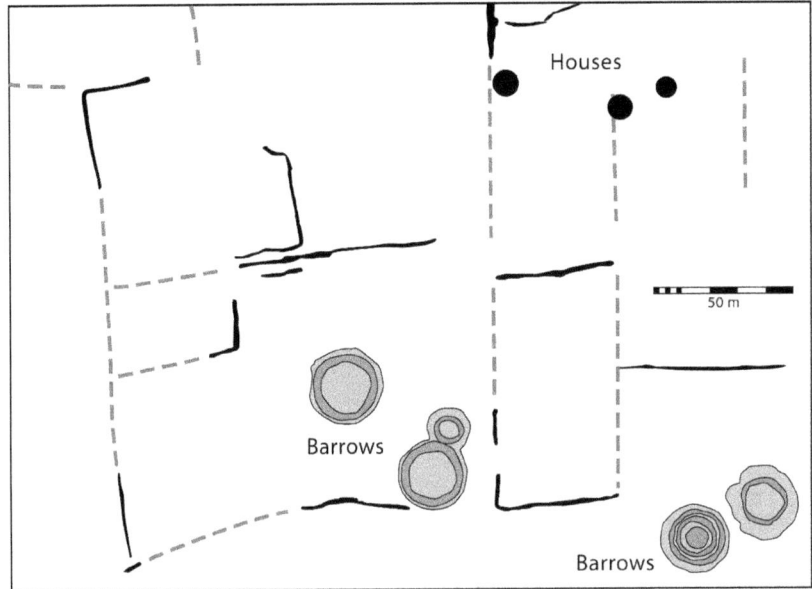

Figure 13 Early Bronze Age barrows and Middle Bronze Age houses and boundaries at Over / Barleycroft, eastern England. Information from Evans (2016).

burial mounds were losing their significance. It was a dramatic change, yet these systems seldom remained in use for very long; afterwards the landscape was organised in other ways (Bradley, Entwistle & Raymond 1994). Williams (2023) characterises the history of the Great Orme copper mine as one of 'boom and bust'. To some extent the same applies to the organisation of the wider landscape, but with an important difference. The copper mine was situated on the coast of upland Britain, but virtually all the enclosed land was in the south and east, in the regions facing Continental Europe. Farming may have changed across a wider area, but it was not accompanied by such a radical reorganisation.

The situation was similar in Ireland where settlements of this date are common, but regular field systems are rare. On the other hand, 'Celtic Fields' are known in north Germany, Belgium, the Netherlands, and South Scandinavia (Arnoldussen, Johnston & Løvschal 2021). They are defined by banks of windblown soil, although settlement excavations have identified other divisions marked by wooden fences. Their layout may not have been as stable as that of their English counterparts, but they conformed to a similar template and seem to have had longer histories. In the Netherlands they originated by 1600 BC. It is justifiable to compare developments across the southern North Sea, but ditched fields have also been identified close to the Channel coast in France.

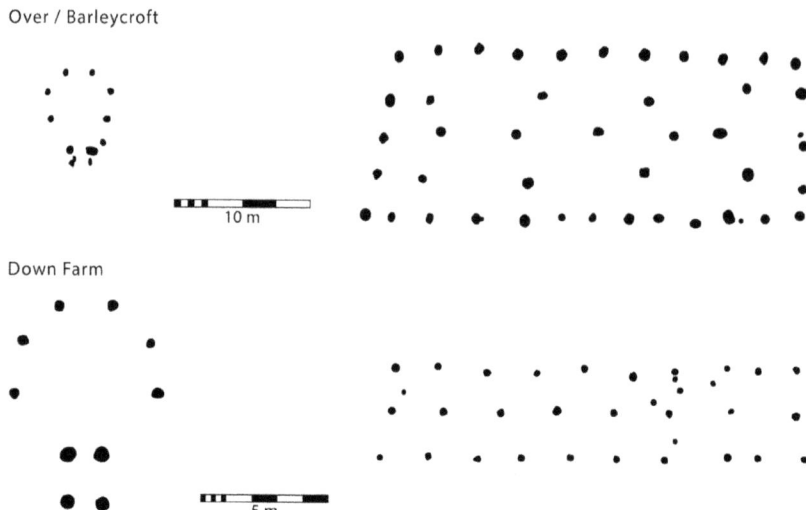

Figure 14 Posthole plans of roundhouses and longhouses at Over / Barleycroft, eastern England, and Down Farm, Wessex. Information from Evans (2016) and Barrett, Bradley and Green (1990)

For a long time, it has been accepted that bronze artefacts were exchanged across the Channel and the North Sea, and more recently researchers have shown that communities on both sides of the water used similar styles of pottery (Lehoërff 2012). Now it appears that new settlements were established in both these areas during the middle and late second millennium BC. There is evidence of increasing sedentism and more sustained food production, but not enough to postulate a single cause for these developments.

The evidence of domestic buildings is more diverse. Those in Britain were roundhouses. By contrast, they are unknown in the Netherlands where three-aisled longhouses were constructed from 1500 BC. Both architectural traditions had deeper roots, but the Dutch examples are associated with a new generation of settlements (Bourgeois & Fontijn 2008). The evidence from two regions departs from this simple outline. Excavations in East Anglia, and to a smaller extent in Wessex, have identified a few rectangular buildings which compare with Continental longhouses although they do not assume identical forms. On the other hand, excavations along the coast of northern France have revealed a series of roundhouses which are like their counterparts in southern England (Figure 14). They are not far from the Channel and contrast with the rectilinear structures found further inland (Bradley, Haselgrove, Vander Linden & Webley 2016, 188–92; Riquier, Maitay, Leroi-Langelin & Maguer 2018).

Whatever the causes – and they may be complex – it seems as if landscapes on both sides of the Channel and the North Sea underwent the same transformation.

Discussion

During this period the relationship between Britain and its neighbours changed. If the Neolithic period had witnessed a gradual shift from integration around 3700 BC to isolation a millennium later, the balance was reversed. By 2500 BC there were important links along the North Sea and the Irish Sea, but the only significant contacts across the water were with the island to the west. The later third millennium BC saw a fresh development as people came from the Continent to settle new land. They crossed the southern part of the North Sea as well as the Channel and travelled up the Atlantic coastline. Their arrival was decisive, but it is too easy to suppose that one population simply replaced another. The first reaction of indigenous communities was to emphasise their own identities by building henges and stone circles on an extravagant scale. Different ways of life and systems of belief coexisted for many years.

People associated with Bell Beakers and metalwork might bury their dead around monuments already constructed by the native inhabitants. The settlers even built similar structures of their own, but the characteristics of insular architecture were never adopted on the Continent. In the same way, Beaker dwellings in Britain and Ireland adhered to insular traditions and were completely unlike those in other regions. It was a contrast that would remain important during later periods. On the other hand, the treatment of the dead was consistent across most parts of Britain and the near-Continent. Burials shared a similar character, and many were associated with the same kinds of mounds and graves.

After the Beaker phase there were growing similarities between the material culture of people living on opposite shores of the Channel and the North Sea. These links extended around the British coast from Cornwall to East Anglia, and along the rim of the Continent from Brittany to the Netherlands. A comparable system may have spanned the Irish Sea. Although certain relationships did change over time, nothing similar can be recognised during the Neolithic period. The closeness of this relationship was entirely new.

Other links reached further inland, although they were obviously selective and connected regions with concentrations of richly furnished burials. Sources of copper, tin and amber were important, and long-distance networks developed to bring them together. Britain played a new role as a major source of tin, and as a consumer of imported bronze and amber. As these networks developed and expanded, the offshore island was drawn into long-distance relationships with Brittany, South Scandinavia, east Central Europe, and even with the Aegean.

If that recalls the traditional notion that the island was on the periphery of a larger system, there were times when the relationship was reversed. Studies of ancient metallurgy show that it happened more than once. From 2200 BC the exploitation of Cornish tin – a comparatively rare resource – allowed insular communities to produce bronze artefacts long before their neighbours on the mainland. It could be exported and would play a vital role over a larger area. Something similar happened again 600 years later when the copper mine at Great Orme supplied some of the occupants of Britain who had previously relied on Continental metals. For 200 years it produced sufficient ore to sustain an export trade, and its products have been identified in Western and Northern Europe.

Between 2500 and 1600 BC settlement sites left little trace in Britain, Ireland and most parts of the near-Continent. The reasons for this are complex, but one possibility is that mobile pastoralism was more important than cultivation. Large concentrations of burial mounds were built in areas of grazing land. When that changed, lasting settlements, houses, and field systems were established. It happened around 1600 BC in different parts of Britain and mainland Europe, although the reasons for this development are not entirely clear. It had always been accepted that communities on opposite sides of the Channel and the North Sea exchanged bronze tools, weapons, and ornaments. They also made ceramics of similar forms, but the results of excavation show that the landscapes in these areas experienced a similar transformation. Although there were important contrasts between styles of domestic architecture, communities who faced one another across the sea came to have much in common. There is very little to suggest British isolation.

It was not true everywhere. The development of stronger relationships between Britain and Continental Europe focused on the south and east of the island where people could travel shorter distances by sea. The point has an important corollary. As these connections intensified, there were fewer new developments in the north. Indeed, by 1600 BC there was an important distinction between areas with contacts in mainland Europe, and those where communities still adhered to local norms (Bradley & Nimura 2016). Some people maintained their links across the Irish Sea, but others became more isolated. That was to change during the first millennium BC.

4 Questions of Time and Space (1200–54 BC)

There are general accounts of Bronze and Iron Age Europe and more detailed studies of prehistoric Britain. The difficulty is relating them to one another. Did important developments extend across large areas, or is it necessary to treat the offshore island separately from the mainland? It is challenging to establish meaningful temporal divisions and even more difficult to work at the right geographical scale. Each part of this account discusses insular developments before considering them in their European contexts.

Histories

Questions of chronology dominated twentieth century research, and some remain unanswered even now. Terminology is revealing. The Three Age System was based on the classification of artefacts according to styles and raw materials. This method has always given problems. A recent find illustrates the point – the axes in one of the latest and largest bronze hoards in Britain were coloured so that they would resemble objects made of iron (Roberts et al. 2015).

Metalwork was not commonly deposited on living sites, and groups of associated artefacts were often discovered in isolation: in rivers, hoards, or Continental graves. It was hard to relate these objects to the settlements that provided the most useful source of information. The British evidence presented a special problem. Field systems first appeared whilst Early Bronze Age barrows were still being built, yet some of the new elements proved unexpectedly short-lived. The domestic landscape had seen many changes by 1200 BC, but some of its characteristic features remained important after 800 BC and even continued into an 'Early' or 'Earliest Iron Age'.

Insular Developments

Even so there were important differences between the practices adopted before 1200 BC, and subsequent developments in Britain.

Existing Features (1200–800 BC)

An initial period saw the intensification of existing features. Deposits of metalwork in dry ground played an increasing role (Bradley 2017). Some objects were newly made, but many showed signs of use. Numerous hoards were associated with metal production, but the transformation of the raw material was not a simple process. The objects in these collections had been fractured with considerable force and certain parts of these artefacts were represented at the expense of others (Knight 2021). Ornaments might also be deposited in wetlands, and weapons in rivers. Swords showed signs of use and repair and some of those in the Thames had been damaged for a second time before they entered the water (York 2002). These practices began during earlier phases but became increasingly important. There were two concentrations of late bronze hoards. Their distributions focussed on the estuaries of the Thames and the Severn: 'the mouths of two noble rivers' in Gildas's description of Britain (Griffiths 2023: figure 5).

Domestic sites resembled those of the previous period but developed in different ways. The best-preserved settlement was at Must Farm in eastern England where the houses and their contents survived almost intact (Knight et al. 2024). Unlike earlier examples, individual roundhouses were built in the same positions as their predecessors, and domestic sites could contain more buildings. Other elements became less common. That applied to co-axial field systems, which often went out of use (Yates 2007). There were few barrows or flat cemeteries, although deposits within the settlements included pieces of cremated bone (Brudnell & Cooper 2008). They did not receive special treatment. Human and animal remains were deposited in waterholes and wells.

New Elements (1200–800 BC)

New features developed and remained in use for a long time. Among them were novel kinds of land boundary: linear ditches and pit alignments. Features of this kind cut across the field systems in lowland Britain (Bradley, Entwistle & Raymond 1994). The new divisions enclosed larger areas than before, and their overall distribution extended from river valleys in the south as far as the borders between England, Wales, and Scotland. They do not seem to have been established simultaneously and are poorly dated.

Among them were the linear earthworks of northeast England which remained important from the Late Bronze Age to the middle of the Iron Age: a period of 500 years. One site illustrates a fresh development. At Thwing a massive circular enclosure was constructed near the point where several of these boundaries met. It resembled a Neolithic henge but had a timber-revetted rampart. In its centre was a wooden building like an enormous roundhouse, associated with a deposit of cremated bone (Manby, King & Vyner 2003: 65–8).

Such monuments have become known as *ringworks* (Figure 15). Their chronology seems to be confined to the early first millennium BC (Johnston 2021: 20–6). The first accounts supposed that their distribution was limited to southern and eastern England, with an emphasis on the Thames Estuary and the North Sea. That is no longer true, and similar monuments have been identified in regions further west. Not all were precisely circular; others were oval or even square. In some cases, a large roundhouse faced the entrance. These monuments could be surrounded by open settlements.

They shared other features. Some sites provide evidence of metalworking, including the production of ornaments and weapons. There were deposits of

Insularity and Identity 45

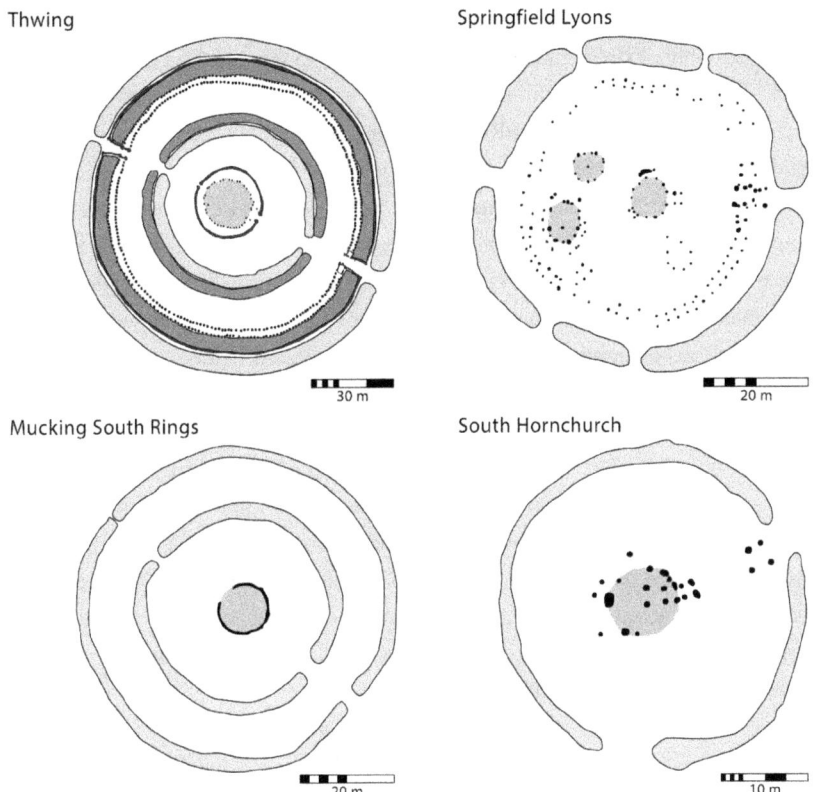

Figure 15 Outline plans of four ringworks. Information from Bradley (2019).

finished objects and clay moulds, and a few ringworks contained cremation burials. They were also associated with fine pottery and with perforated ceramic slabs that may have played a role in the preparation of food (Champion 2014). It is likely that such sites had a special role (Johnston 2021: 20–6). The activities which took place there included feasting and craft production.

The assemblages from these ringworks recall another development. A series of middens appeared at about the same time (Waddington et al. 2019; McOmish 2020). Some were very extensive and contained extraordinary quantities of artefacts, faunal remains, and evidence of artefact manufacture. Normally this material would have been spread on cultivated land, but here it was allowed to accumulate until it formed a mound. The main component of these deposits was animal dung. The distribution of sites extended from southeast England to south Wales.

It is difficult to decide whether these middens were associated with dwellings. Some covered the remains of roundhouses and in one case domestic buildings were identified nearby. The 'dark earth' of which the deposits were composed included patches of cobbles, ovens, and hearths. Wooden structures might also have existed but could be impossible to recognise in deposits of this kind. The problem is familiar from urban archaeology where similar layers accumulated over the sites of Roman towns. Again, they were associated with artefacts suggesting continued occupation.

The prehistoric middens contained an unprecedented quantity of artefacts, human remains, and animal bones. There were unusual levels of craft production which included metalworking and the weaving of textiles. One idea is that these places were where special objects were made and exchanged. The vast accumulations of dung suggest that livestock changed hands, too. The hearths and ovens may provide evidence of feasting, but it was not the only function of these sites.

A few middens were more distinctive. They were located by potential landing places on the seashore or along major rivers. The coastal sites show the same emphasis on metal production and include examples beside a sheltered route leading between the Channel, the Thames Estuary, and the North Sea. They featured a series of earthworks comparable with ringworks (McKinley et al. 2014). Middens have been identified on other islands in rivers with concentrations of metal finds (Needham 1991).

Transitions (800–400 BC)

The chronology of the middens has been investigated in detail and this research shows that they were not an exclusively Bronze Age phenomenon. A new study based on radiocarbon dating suggests that they were forming by 1000 BC, but their chronologies varied. Some were employed for short periods, but others remained in use much longer. At the example studied in most detail the rate of deposition increased during the Early Iron Age (Waddington et al. 2019).

Although Cunliffe (2005) distinguishes between an 'Earliest Iron Age' from 800 to 600 BC and an 'Early Iron Age' which ended about 400 BC, it is difficult to study the period transition. There are problems calibrating radiocarbon dates during these phases, and there may never have been the abrupt change predicated by the Three Age Model. Bronze and iron were very different substances and were worked in completely different ways (Garrow & Gosden 2012: 14–21). To treat both in the same terms could be anachronistic.

It is hard to work out how one material replaced the other. There is no doubt that the supply of metal did change, but it is unwise to measure it by the number of artefacts that survive today (Needham 2007). Their frequency must have been influenced by past conventions concerning their deposition (or non-deposition), and these remain entirely conjectural. Other factors may be more informative: the evidence of bronze working provided by scrap hoards and metal analysis; the direct indications of bronze and iron production documented by finds of slag, furnaces, and moulds. There are also the results of fieldwork at copper mines on the Continent. The sources of ore changed as individual sites went out of use (O'Brien 2015), and the distributions of finished artefacts certainly suggest that they were brought from the mainland along separate routes.

The argument that the supply of materials came under pressure depends on the evidence of recycling identified by metal analysis. Another indication of a reduced supply is the peak of 'metalworking hoards' towards the end of the Bronze Age, but when the number of deposits fell, they still featured in a few parts of Britain, including Cornwall, Wessex, and East Anglia (Griffiths 2023).

It is equally important is to consider early ironworking. Again, the evidence is limited. There are finds of slag from the upper layers of middens in Wessex, and others come from settlement excavations. There are rare instances in which the established forms of bronze artefacts were reproduced in iron or where objects combined both materials. Otherwise finds of early ironwork are scarcely more common than objects made of bronze. One implication is that neither was widely available, but there is an obvious alternative to this argument – perhaps they were not deposited in the ground. That remains a possibility, but before the fifth century BC metalwork need not have been as significant as the period labels suggest.

Existing Features (800–400 BC)

Some practices remained important up to 400 BC and possibly after that time. They have already been introduced in this account, but it is important to emphasise their longevity. Many were related to land use, but others were more arcane.

The boundary ditches and pit alignments established in the previous phase remained particularly significant. In some cases, they were linked to new settlements, and other occupation sites developed within the areas they enclosed. These divisions were maintained and reconfigured, and in Wessex a few defended enclosures developed in the places where they converged. It is not clear how long this way of organising the landscape retained its influence, but it must have been before a new generation of field systems was established in the late first millennium BC.

Another development that continued was the deposition of weapons in rivers (Bradley 2017). Whatever its explanation, this practice was maintained in some regions after the burial of dryland hoards had diminished or disappeared in others. Fewer artefacts were involved, and they are found in fewer places. For example, their distribution contracted to one section of the Thames (Cunliffe 2005: figure 20.19), although finds of similar character have been recorded elsewhere. It was only during the late pre-Roman period that they would approach their former frequency.

Other developments ended during this period. There is little evidence that open air middens were used so intensively. Quantities of artefacts, animal bones and human bodies accumulated throughout the Iron Age, but by 400 BC they were being placed in disused storage pits – because they were concealed, there might have been less emphasis on display (Williams 2003). A similar consideration applied to domestic architecture. Ringworks were used until about 700 BC but were no longer built after that time. On the other hand, conspicuous roundhouses like those associated with these monuments were still constructed. They were not common, but their distribution extended from open settlements to a small number of early hillforts. They were comparatively short-lived as later domestic buildings were smaller and much more uniform in plan and construction (Sharples 2010: 226–31).

New Elements (800–400 BC)

It is difficult to identify new components with the same amount of confidence. The origins of British hillforts present a problem. Some of the radiocarbon samples associated with their defences might be residual as many sites had already been open settlements or had been enclosed by palisades. In the same way, the buildings inside them need not date from the same phase as the defences. Certain hills were already important because hoards of bronze metalwork had been buried there, but it is not known whether the sites were occupied at the time. A number of hillforts must have originated in the Late Bronze Age for their ramparts had the same structure as those at several ringworks, but it is too soon to estimate how many began life at that time. Most of the dating evidence is unsatisfactory and some of the first hillforts went out of use after the eighth century BC (Lock & Ralston 2022: 312–68). At present the most convincing information comes from western and northern Britain.

Early hillforts were mostly used in the same ways. Some were exceptionally extensive, yet their earthwork boundaries might be insubstantial. Not all of them contained many buildings; there were roundhouses, but the commonest structures inside them were raised granaries (Cunliffe 2005: 378–84). Both were established in open settlements. Grain silos were uncommon in an initial phase although their frequency increased later. Not all the houses need have been occupied all year and it is likely that certain sites were used on an occasional basis. In a few cases early hillforts were destroyed by fire. Again, this was most common in the north and west.

In lowland areas it can be difficult to distinguish these monuments from simpler enclosures of the same date and to some extent the difference may be due to accidents of survival; there could have been a continuum rather than a hierarchy. In any case the ratio of open sites to enclosed settlements was unstable. Individual settlements could shift between these forms, and any general patterns must be established on a local basis. What is obvious is that occupation sites of all kinds were associated with intensive mixed farming and that their number was increasing; in some cases that process had started during the previous period. Domestic sites could be surprisingly close together and it is possible that individual examples replaced one another. There were few variations between their contents – or between the finds from these sites and those from early hillforts – and there is nothing to indicate overt distinctions of status. The new settlements appear to have been largely self-sufficient.

It is hard to identify general trends when there were so many local variations, but even that observation is revealing. Individual styles of Early Iron Age pottery were distributed across smaller areas than those of Late Bronze Age metalwork and there appear to have been clear divisions between them (Cunliffe 2005: 70–124). Compared with the previous period, the centre of gravity seems to have shifted from places connected to the coast. Settlements were more widely distributed and there was greater diversity.

A European Setting

An Initial Phase (1200–800 BC)

Perhaps these developments operated on two levels. They were not necessarily related to differences of status, although Bronze Age and Iron Age communities are sometimes characterised as chiefdoms (Ling, Earle & Kristiansen 2018). The most immediate contrast is between routine practices and those undertaken with greater formality. Food production and metalworking were ritualised in some contexts and not in others.

The information varies at different geographical scales. In the first part of this sequence the largest entities were the Urnfield Culture and the Atlantic Bronze Age (Figure 16). Their distributions complemented one another on the mainland, and each impinged on the archaeology of Britain. Both terms describe widely distributed features of societies that were diverse at a more local level. The Urnfield Culture took its name from a distinctive mortuary rite, although new research recognises considerable variety in its expression and development (Sørensen & Rebay-Salisbury 2023). The alternative is to emphasise its

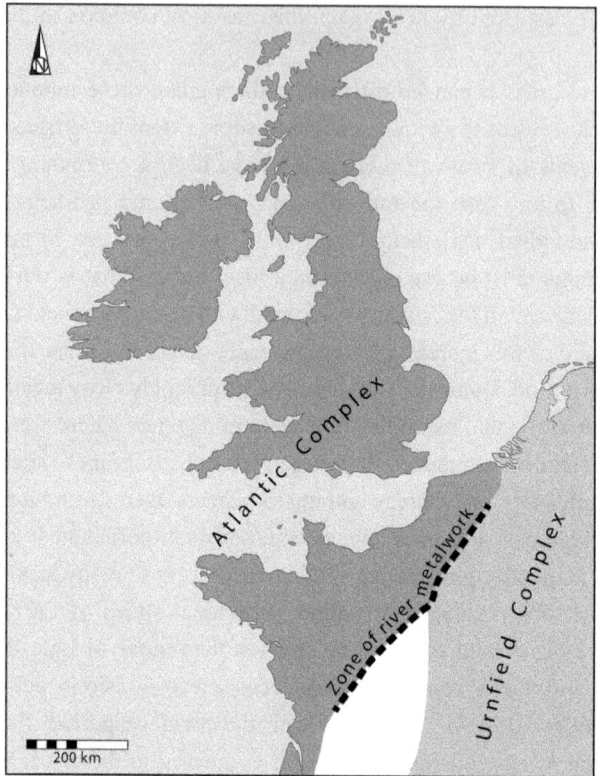

Figure 16 The relationship between the Urnfield and Atlantic zones, and the concentration of river metalwork in between them.

geographical extent, and this complex has also been called the *Rhine / Swiss / Eastern French* or *North Alpine* tradition. The term *Atlantic Bronze Age* covers almost as many related phenomena, but much depends on whether it is defined by artefact styles, cultural practices, or the movement of raw materials (Ruiz-Gálvez 1998; Milcent 2012). Continental chronology places the beginning of the Urnfield Culture in the thirteenth century BC, but it did not extend to the offshore island. The Atlantic Bronze Age began at about the same time and did incorporate Britain and Ireland. Such contacts were not new as there had been close connections between north-west France and Wessex during the Early Bronze Age.

Both complexes can be considered on two levels. The most basic was the domestic sphere. Although the number of settlements increased, there were few entirely new developments. Despite changes of domestic architecture, settlements remained dispersed, and some could be occupied for short periods. The distinction between insular roundhouses and rectangular dwellings on the

Continent was maintained. So was the construction of circular buildings near the north coast of France (Riquier, Maitay, Leroi-Langelin & Maguer 2018). Field systems remained in use in the Low Countries but in England, they were replaced by new land divisions; longer boundaries were also established in parts of mainland Europe (Løvschal 2014). Small burial mounds and flat cemeteries are recorded on the near-Continent, but in Britain they were virtually absent. On the other hand, fragments of cremated human bone are represented at settlements in both regions. Bronze hoards were another common element and, as in the previous phase, domestic artefacts assumed similar forms on both sides of the Channel and the southern part of the North Sea. The same applies to distinctive styles of fine metalwork (Lehöerff 2012). Most of the same features connected Britain with Ireland.

There were more significant developments at a second level. On the Continent the distinction between the Atlantic Bronze Age and the Urnfield complex depends on mortuary rites and metalwork. The inhabitants of Britain drew on both traditions but did not place the same emphasis on the dead. Some of the new developments were widely shared. They included new practices as well as the elaboration of existing ones.

The treatment of metalwork raises important issues. There was an obvious distinction between the deposition of weapons in water and their presence in graves. These practices had mutually exclusive distributions and the placing of swords in rivers has been interpreted as a kind of mortuary rite performed in regions where furnished burials were absent (Bradley 2017: 152–4). There was an obvious contrast between their association with the dead in Central Europe and their representation in other contexts further to the north. River metalwork features on both sides of the Channel. The concentration of swords and spears in the Thames has direct equivalents in rivers like the Rhine and the Seine. The condition of these artefacts shows that they had been employed in combat: another feature that was shared between Britain and the mainland. A further characteristic is that similar types of weapons were distributed over considerable areas, although local conventions influenced the decision about where or when to deposit them.

Some practices had a more restricted currency. In the Atlantic Bronze Age finds of weapons are complemented by a specialised assemblage associated with the provision of food and drink (Needham & Bowman 2005; Milcent 2012). It featured buckets, cauldrons, flesh hooks, and spits which were distributed from Portugal in the south to Ireland and Scotland in the north. Their distribution did not impinge on the regions within the Urnfield tradition. In fact, the geographical division between those complexes was marked by some early hillforts and unusually large or rich settlements (Peake 2020). It also included finds of river metalwork. One possibility is that they were deposited in a buffer zone during times of conflict.

For many years such metalwork has engaged the interest of specialists, but there is an important distinction between their detailed analyses and the broader categories to which the objects belonged. Despite the differences between distinct kinds of swords, spears, and shields, all had similar connotations and would have featured in armed conflict, whether actual or ceremonial. In the same way, the precise forms of cauldrons and flesh hooks might have been less significant than their association with large gatherings of people and the conspicuous consumption of food. Again, there was an emphasis on display which was shared between people on the Continent and the inhabitants of Britain.

These elements are evidenced in other ways. Weapons were sometimes made at hillforts or ringworks in Britain where the earthwork boundary provided another kind of protection. Such enclosures were not built simply for show, as a few defended sites in the west and north were destroyed by fire. That may be significant as they were among the earliest monuments of their kind. Their construction and use might have been influenced by developments across the water in Ireland where hillforts were a feature of the early first millennium and were not used afterwards (O'Brien & O'Driscoll 2017). There were others on the near-Continent and those in northern France were of similar age to those in Britain (Delrieu 2013; Krausz 2019). More is known about their defences than the ways in which they were used. Their ramparts took the same form at insular hillforts and ringworks; other ringworks were represented in Ireland, France and Germany; an example in Normandy was associated with a settlement of roundhouses (Mare et al. 2018).

Middens were associated with the British ringworks as well as early hillforts and open sites. They were associated with craft production and provided evidence of feasts. They have been treated as an insular phenomenon, but again they compare with evidence from western France and Ireland. The unenclosed middens in England are very like those excavated inside the Irish promontory fort of Dún Aonghasa (Cotter 2012) and on the island of Ouessant off the west coast of France (Le Bihan & Villard 2010).

Even if Britain was on the outer edge of Europe, its occupants were closely connected with those of the Continent. That applied to communities from the north of Scotland to the south of England, and along both the east and west coasts of the island. They engaged in similar practices and had similar preoccupations, from the routines of domestic life to lavish feasts and episodes of violence. When Early Bronze Age communities had formed long-distance alliances they were with the occupants of a few distant areas – the links between Wessex, Brittany, the Únětice sphere, and the Aegean provide the obvious examples. There had been connections across the Channel or the southern part of the North Sea, but those with more remote areas were *focused* and *specific*. During the period considered here socio-political relations became more expansive and took a different form.

The Transition (800–400 BC)

It is easy to interpret the adoption of iron according to the assumptions of the Three Age model, but there are risks in doing so. Although this scheme was invented as a way of ordering a museum collection, it soon came under the influence of wider notions of progress and technological efficiency. They may not have been so relevant to prehistory.

Discussions usually focus on the dual role of bronze. It could be used to make weapons and personal ornaments but also provided many of the tools employed in daily life. That statement overlooks a significant element. Bronze was an alloy of different materials, obtained with considerable effort from a limited number of sources and sometimes brought together over long distances. Even when it was recycled, it was worked by specialised processes which have been compared with magic. Iron, on the other hand, was transformed by other methods and could be found more widely. Was it because it lacked the special connotations of bronze that it took so long to be accepted? Iron could have been used to make tools and weapons, yet for many years the appropriate technology was known, available and little used (Champion 2023). A helpful comparison is with the circulation of Irish gold which was used to make personal jewellery during the same period. It cannot have been by chance that its use declined simultaneously with that of bronze (Eogan 1994).

It is difficult to distinguish between cause and effect. One model focuses on the *availability* of bronze and suggests that its movement in Western and Northern Europe was managed by an elite – social position depended on controlling access to a vital but widely distributed material. Advocates of this interpretation consider that it was obtained from a few restricted areas and study how those sources changed over time. They postulate the development of 'maritime chiefdoms' along the coast (Ling, Earle & Kristiansen 2018). It is true that there was a significant development at this time. Less new material might have been available, suggesting a need to recycle metal that was in short supply. The deposition of gold declined at the same time, yet access could never have been subject to the same constraints. Perhaps it lost its significance as a social currency *because long-distance alliances were already breaking down*.

This is not the place to investigate the reasons why those networks changed, but the effects of such developments are obvious. New research suggests that

Central Europe lost its dominant position as a source of copper, first to the Italian Alps and then to southern Spain (Ling et al. 2024). The sources of the metal became increasingly distant from the regions where their products were consumed. Cornish tin remained important, and the Atlantic Bronze Age played a greater part than ever before. But there was a potential problem because such a system was more extended than the networks it replaced. At its extreme, it reached from Iberia and the west Mediterranean as far as Scandinavia and for that reason, it would have become increasingly vulnerable. This was a period in which competitive display and conspicuous consumption played a major part and the evidence of damaged weapons and burnt fortifications shows how easily those processes could lead to conflicts. Long-distance connections might have been disrupted, and if relations became particularly unstable there would have been no way of restoring them. The British evidence indicates such a period of fragmentation. There was a new emphasis on local developments rather than long-distance links.

The end of the Atlantic Bronze Age affected many communities in northwest Europe who must have shared in its undramatic aftermath (Schumann & van der Vaart-Verschoof 2017). They do not feature prominently in general accounts of the Iron Age. That is because of another change in networks of alliance and exchange. In the sixth and fifth centuries BC societies in the Mediterranean interacted with local elites in southern Germany and central France. The principal connections were through Massalia (modern Marseilles) and are evidenced by the growth of important hillforts and associated settlements (*Fürstensitze*). It is likely that the power of these communities depended on control over land and food production and that access to exotic imports was a subsequent development (Fernández-Götz & Ralston 2017). But when it did happen, the inhabitants drew on foreign styles of architecture and in their funeral rites they even adopted a version of the Classical *symposium*. They commemorated their dead by filling their graves with luxuries imported from the south. After the power of these communities declined in the fifth century BC similar relationships were established in neighbouring regions. In this case, the main evidence comes from cemeteries rather than settlements (Demoule 1999).

Such evidence is already well known, and only one point is relevant to this account of Britain and its neighbours. These regions were *almost entirely beyond* the areas affected by such dramatic developments (Milcent 2006), and, with local exceptions in the southern Netherlands (Fontijn & Fokkens 2007), their archaeologies lack such distinctive elements. The inhabitants had been among the last to adopt iron on a significant scale, and during the fourth and third centuries BC they played no part in the Celtic migrations that extended across other parts of Europe.

Endings (400–54 BC)

This account of British prehistory will end at the point when Julius Caesar twice invaded England. His reasons for doing so evoke two themes of this Element. One of his motives was public and explicit, but the other can only be understood in terms of Classical beliefs. Both introduce ideas which will feature in the remaining part of this section.

Britain occupied a special place in the ancient world. According to a recent commentator, 'the sea and the land lying within it had a numinous quality that elevated campaigning to a magical act' (Hingley 2022: 4). That was because people believed that the earth was surrounded by a continuous body of water – Oceanus – which was both a geographical element and a divinity. Caesar was emulating Alexander the Great who made sacrifices to Oceanus before embarking on his campaigns.

At the same time, he needed to justify his invasion to his supporters and opponents in Rome. He did so by reporting that the inhabitants of this remote island had sent warriors to reinforce native resistance to his invasion of Gaul. Thus, he had two reasons for coming to Britain. It was a mysterious place beyond the familiar world, and in doing so he was confronting a supernatural power. At the same time, he claimed that the inhabitants of Britain were allies of his adversaries on the mainland. This section will consider some of the evidence for those connections.

Insular Developments and Their Wider Relationships

Regional Patterning

In 400 BC Britain was outside the main currents in Iron Age Europe. It shared features with its neighbours to the south and east – styles of everyday artefacts, similar settlement patterns and methods of food production – but there are few indications of the long-distance networks that were so important during earlier periods (Lehoërff, Bourgeois, Clark & Talon 2012; Webley 2015). How did the insular sequence develop and how were Continental elements assimilated by the time of Caesar's invasion?

There were many more settlements, and their distribution extended into regions that had not been inhabited on a significant scale before. The number of new sites is reflected by a growing impact on the landscape. Local traditions had been developing since the period of fragmentation that began around 800 BC, but one feature is particularly striking. Now large parts of the British landscape were divided between three zones in each of which settlement took different forms. Each of them shared characteristics with the nearest parts of the Continent (Figure 17; Cunliffe 2005: figure 21.6).

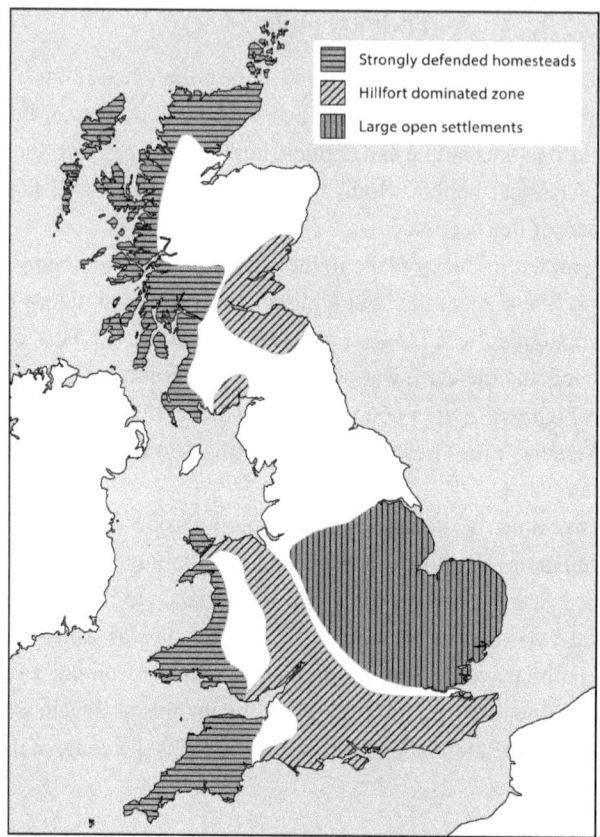

Figure 17 Regional traditions of settlement in Britain in the mid second century BC. Information from Bradley (2019).

One contained concentrations of major hillforts. Between 400 BC and the second or first centuries BC their number fell, and certain locations assumed a dominant position (Figure 18). They were more widely spaced than their predecessors and many commanded specific territories. The construction of their defences required a large labour force whose involvement might have helped to build stronger bonds within the community (Sharples 2010). The term hillfort is a misnomer. Although occasional examples were attacked or destroyed, it did not happen often – they were not military architecture. The features inside them were simple roundhouses, granaries, and storage pits. A few included shrines. Their contents of hillforts were like those of other sites, but certain contrasts can be recognised between them. They provide more evidence of rituals, and the houses there could be less robust than those in other places. Storage structures often outnumbered domestic dwellings. Their relationship with surrounding settlements changed and in Wessex people may have

Figure 18 Uffington Castle hillfort. Photograph: Creative Commons. Credit: Dave Price

lived there all year round when other places were abandoned (Davis 2013). In their final phases large hillforts became hill towns (Sharples 2014), but some of those in the north were in such exposed positions that they may have been occupied only seasonally. Many hillforts in lowland England went out of use by the first century BC (Fitzpatrick, Haselgrove & Lowther 2023). There is little to suggest that they were associated with a social elite. Instead, they might have been where assemblies took place and communal decisions were made. Although Irish hillforts went out of use during the Late Bronze Age, the distribution of Iron Age monuments extended across the Channel from England into northern France, though few have been investigated on a large scale (Krausz 2019).

Open settlements formed a second group. In Britain they were on lower ground, especially in the east (Thomas 2010). They were of various sizes, and many were associated with land divisions of the kinds considered earlier. The occupied area could include separate compounds which might have developed incrementally as the inhabitants of different sites chose to join a larger community. These sites contained numerous roundhouses as well as pits and raised storehouses. Several included shrines like those at hillforts. The open settlements provide evidence of similar practices to defended sites and contain human and animal burials within abandoned grain silos. There is evidence of feasting and craft production, and, like the hillforts of the same period, occasional examples feature separate zones of houses and granaries (Thomas 2010). Open settlements are best known from surface finds (often found by metal detectorists) or from partial excavation, but it is obvious that the largest examples in eastern England were associated with richer collections of artefacts than any other sites of the same date. This is where differences of status may be most apparent. Such settlements can be compared with extensive Iron Age sites on the opposite side of the North Sea, although the contrast between roundhouses and longhouses was maintained throughout this period.

A third important element was a distribution of small circular structures of various kinds whose distribution extended along the west coast of Britain (Cunliffe 2001b; Henderson 2007). They took many different forms, from the small circular stone or earthwork enclosures called rounds, raths or duns, to monumental roundhouses or circular towers which were peculiar to Scotland. Sites of most kinds were associated with groups of dwellings, but others existed on their own. They contrast with the other two traditions since storage pits were unimportant. Granaries are rare, but at sites in southwest England and northern Scotland individual dwellings were associated with the underground cellars known as souterrains. Many small circular monuments were near the sea, and it is not surprising that they share this feature with similar structures extending along the Atlantic coast from Iberia to Brittany. The parallels between them are striking. That is particularly true of Breton cliff castles and souterrains, and stone roundhouses in Spain and Portugal.

Thus, the main patterns identified in the British landscape share features with those in parts of Continental Europe: northern France in the case of hillforts; the open settlements of the Low Countries; and the small circular structures distributed along the fringe of Atlantic Europe. Distinctions between Britain and the Continent were becoming less clear-cut. But they had their limits. Larger agglomerated settlements – *oppida* – were developing in Continental Europe yet this process was only beginning in Britain at the time of Caesar's invasion (Fichtl 2005; Fernández-Götz 2019; Krausz 2019). His references to the strongholds of local leaders suggest that they were simply hillforts. Other connections are emphasised by finds of portable objects which must have passed between Britain and the mainland. But there were more specific links, and they are considered in the next section. They shed light on the cross-Channel alliances that Caesar found so troublesome.

New Developments

Four new developments illustrate the changing relationship between Britain and Continental Europe: the introduction of Celtic Art; the choice of special places for maritime trade; the adoption of burial practices similar to those employed on the mainland; and the first use of coins.

La Tène art was first characterised by the decorated metalwork associated with a deposit in Switzerland which could have formed after a battle (Kaesar 2022). The definition has extended to cover ceramic decoration, coins and sculptures, but in Britain it is the fine metalwork that has attracted most attention. For many years it was assigned to a later phase than its counterparts on the mainland (Jope 2000), but this was simply an example of the time lag between Continental and insular chronologies discussed in the first part of this Element. New research employing radiocarbon dating has corrected the mistake and shows that this distinctive visual culture was adopted in Britain from the fourth century BC, simultaneously with its development on the mainland (Garrow, Gosden, Hill & Bronk Ramsay 2009; Garrow & Gosden 2012). Its repertoire extended from pins, brooches and torcs, to cauldrons, horse harness, swords with decorated scabbards, shields, and spears. Together they suggest a growing emphasis on warfare, riding and feasting, not unlike the practices associated with the Atlantic Bronze Age hundreds of years before, but there is little to suggest that many of these items were imports. Instead, they indicate that insular communities were adopting similar artefacts and practices to people in other parts of Europe. Links with Ireland were particularly important (Raftery 1984).

Many of the more elaborate items must have been made by specialists working for a patron; these objects also employed non-local materials. There were deposits of fine metalwork, including the hoards from an important sanctuary at Snettisham in eastern England (Farley & Joy 2024). A few production sites have also been discovered. The clearest evidence that other artefacts were introduced by sea – along the English coast or between Britain and the Continent – comes from a series of specialised sites on the ancient shoreline. Although they resemble those used during earlier periods, they were a largely new development. In the fourth century BC the Greek traveller Pytheas visited the offshore island of Ictis where foreign traders obtained tin from the inhabitants of southwest England (Cunliffe 2001a). There were other trading places along the east coast, but the most significant were in southern Wessex where timber jetties were built in Poole Harbour during the second century BC (Wilkes, Pitman, Randall & Brown 2021). In the early first century BC another port developed not far away at Hengistbury Head (Figure 19; Cunliffe 1987). It was through this site that metals were exported to the Continent and exotic commodities, including wine, were brought to southern England. Such sites demonstrate how far British insularity was breaking down.

Figure 19 Christchurch Harbour viewed from Hengistbury Head. Photograph: Richard Bradley

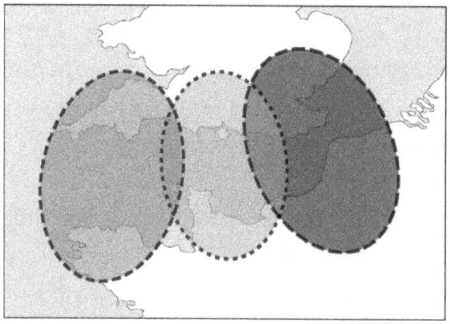

Figure 20 Three traditions of Le Tène burials extending across the Channel. Information from Vannier (2020)

Distinctive kinds of graves and cemeteries illustrate the closeness between insular societies and those on the mainland (Figure 20). Certain practices were shared between neighbouring parts of Britain and Continental Europe (Lamb 2022). Although there has been an emphasis on formal graves, the commonest and most widely distributed deposits are unburnt bodies in storage pits (Delattre 2000; Williams 2003). They were increasingly abundant in settlements of the later first millennium BC and were shared between people in southern England and the near-Continent. From about 450 BC they were complemented by more formal traditions shared by communities on opposite shores of the Channel (Vannier 2020).

In complete contrast, a group of cemeteries in northeast England developed about 200 BC (Giles 2012). It was characterised by many square

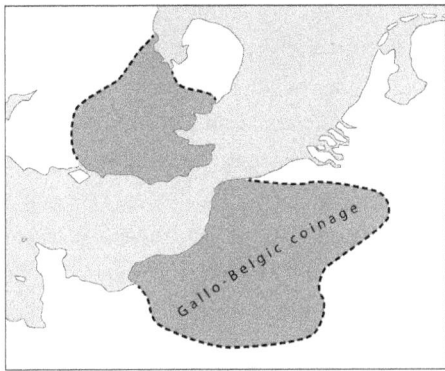

Figure 21 Distribution of early gold coins shared between Britain and Continental Europe

barrows and a series of inhumation burials. Occasionally bodies were placed in dismantled vehicles – 'chariots' – while some of the later graves on these sites contained the bodies of men accompanied by weapons. These sites produce artefacts embellished in La Tène style, and the layout of these cemeteries recalls examples in mainland Europe where they are widely distributed; the closest comparisons are with northern France, but there may be differences of date. Although it is tempting to postulate immigration from that region, the case is far from clear. The most distinctive grave goods were influenced by Continental designs but were local copies of foreign artefacts. Bodies were laid out according to insular norms, and these cemeteries were associated with groups of roundhouses of British type. There must have been connections between distant regions, but their character has still to be determined.

A final indication of changing relationships between Britain and the Continent is the introduction of coins. In north-west Europe they were first minted in the third century BC, and their introduction to southern England followed in the middle of the second century BC. The early issues were mainly of gold (Figure 21; Creighton 2000). Their frequency increased at the time when Caesar invaded Gaul and it seems likely that the supply increased as a way of paying mercenaries – the growing number of coins could be explained by British involvement in the conflict. Their weights and raw materials were closely related to those of personal ornaments embellished in a style of Celtic Art (Farley and Joy 2024). Coin distributions are significant, too. A few came from Brittany, perhaps through Hengistbury Head, but most of the others are described as 'Gallo-Belgic' because they originated in the region supposedly occupied by the Continental Belgae; the earliest examples are distributed across southeast England. The terminology is revealing as it suggests that they circulated on both sides of the Channel.

There are other indications of an increasingly close relationship between the inhabitants of Britain and people on the Continent and these are simply examples that illustrate a wider process. Caesar's description of insular society is not consistent with the results of archaeological research and was composed with a Roman audience in mind. But he was probably correct in emphasising the links between the indigenous inhabitants and their neighbours. Although he used the information to justify an unjustifiable war, in this respect his account was accurate.

5 Conclusions – The Known World
History, Language, and Ancient DNA

Insularity and identity feature together in Caesar's description of Britain. At the time of his first expedition in 55 BC he found it difficult to establish the character of the island:

> [He] thought it would be of advantage to him to visit ... to see what its inhabitants were like and to make himself acquainted with the lie of the land, the harbours, and the landing-places ... In the ordinary way traders are the only people to visit Britain, and even they know only that part of the coast which faces Gaul ... He could not ascertain anything about the size of the island, [or] the character and strength of the tribes which inhabited it (*The Conquest of Gaul*, Book IV: 3).

A year later he had more information:

> By far the most civilised inhabitants are those living in Kent (a purely maritime district) ... The interior of Britain is inhabited by people who claim, on the strength of oral tradition, to be aboriginal; the coast [is occupied] by Belgic immigrants who came to plunder and make war ... and later settled down to till the soil. The population is exceedingly large, the ground thickly studded with homesteads, closely resembling those of the Gauls (*The Conquest of Gaul*, Book V: 1).

The Belgae occupied an area extending inland from the coast between the Rhine and the Seine, but connections of this kind extended further. Caesar said that 'nearly all [the settlers] retain[ed] the names of the tribes from which they originated'. Collis (2003) has discussed the pairing of names between ancient peoples in Britain, Ireland, and the mainland. It applied to the Belgae themselves, whose name was shared between communities in northwest Europe and Wessex, and it was also the case with the Atrebates who were recorded in northern France and southern England (Figure 22). The Parisi, who lived in

Insularity and Identity

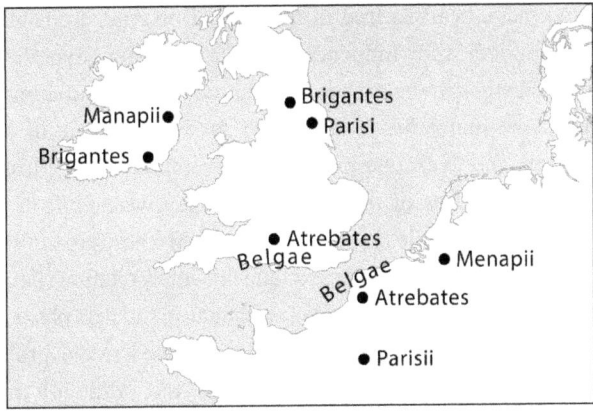

Figure 22 The names shared between peoples in Britain, Ireland and Continental Europe according to Collis (2003)

northeast England, had the same name as another Continental group, and there might have been a similar link between the Brigantes in the north of England and people in southeast Ireland; a further connection was between the Menapii in northeast France and inhabitants of the Irish midlands with the same name. Collis is rightly cautious, but his account points to connections across the Channel and the Irish Sea.

Those connections must have extended to the language people spoke. This is a controversial topic because that language is described as 'Celtic'. The term was coined before prehistoric archaeology developed when it was easy to connect linguistic studies with an indigenous people mentioned by Classical writers (Collis 2003; Pope 2022). The earliest sources – texts, inscriptions, and place names – show that Celtic was spoken from Central Europe to the Atlantic and from Britain and Ireland as far south as the Iberian Peninsula. The language was employed during the pre-Roman period and could well have developed before the Iron Age. It has survived in different forms in Wales, Scotland, Ireland, the Isle of Man, Cornwall, and Brittany, but has been replaced elsewhere.

Linguists do not agree on where Celtic languages first developed. It might have happened in Central Europe or along the Atlantic coastline; a third version favours a source in France (Sims-Williams 2020). They are equally uncertain when that happened, but there was one phase in which archaeological evidence does show close connections between the appropriate regions. This was the Bronze Age between 1300 and 800 BC. Since versions of the same language were shared between Britain and parts of the mainland, there could have been a time when its inhabitants saw themselves as part of a larger community.

That may not have been so true in the Early Iron Age. Ironically, the first studies of that period were influenced by the 'invasion hypothesis' which explained most changes in the archaeological record by postulating periods of settlement from the mainland. It accounted for the presence of artefacts of Continental forms and even interpreted the development of hillforts – either they were the power bases of new leaders, or they were built to protect the natives from attack. It is ironic that the first results of a new project studying the genetics of the prehistoric population exclude this interpretation (Patterson et al. 2022). Rather than showing large-scale settlement in the first phase of the Iron Age, they suggest that parts of England were settled (most probably from France) during the Middle and / or Late Bronze Age. Although this research is at an early stage, the idea is consistent with the evidence of long-distance contacts during those phases.

'In the Shape of a Triangle'

This was Strabo's description of British geography. The island was bounded by three seaways which separated it from Ireland and the Continent. Previous sections have shown that these coasts had different histories from one another. Because separate developments happened along each axis it is unwise to treat Britain as a single unit. A few examples taken from earlier sections illustrate the point.

Links with the Continent were important at certain times and less significant at others. That is clear from the Neolithic sequence. It began in a period of contact with communities in France and the Low Countries, but those connections became less significant as insular traditions developed, and by 3000 BC they had lapsed altogether. The Late Neolithic period saw new developments in Orkney and now the emphasis was almost entirely on connections across the Irish Sea and along the North Sea.

That provides the clearest example of regional differences. The introduction of new people during the Chalcolithic period broke down many of these contrasts and certainly restored relations with mainland Europe. That had happened by the Early Bronze Age, but after that time local alignments became important too. Around the south and east coasts – and subsequently in their hinterland – the landscape was reorganised as new kinds of settlements and territorial divisions developed. They were established in the regions closest to the Continent. During the Atlantic Bronze Age, the movement of metalwork formed another link. But other parts of the island were outside this new system.

Again, such long-distance alignments were vulnerable, and the early Iron Age saw fewer contacts around the coast. Settlements assumed increasingly

Insularity and Identity

local forms and links across the Irish Sea ended for a while. Relations with Continental Europe were eventually reinstated, so that Caesar could comment on the connections between people on opposite sides of the Channel. Even then there was significant diversity. Small circular settlements along the seaways of western Britain shared features with those in Atlantic Europe, but occupation sites of the same date around the east coast had an entirely different character. Insular culture still followed local lines, and so did any relationships with distant areas.

Other observations are important. Communities in northern Britain – especially those living in inland areas – did not play any part in these developments. They had fewer links with the Continent and during the second millennium BC they continued to erect monuments of kinds that had become obsolete in the south; such structures included henges and stone circles. In other respects, their activities anticipated innovations in other regions. They occupied substantial timber roundhouses which resemble those built in lowland England several centuries later.

That summary offers a terrestrial perspective, but maritime archaeology suggests a different approach. Two features are especially important here (Figure 23). The first is the pivotal role played by the regions in which sea

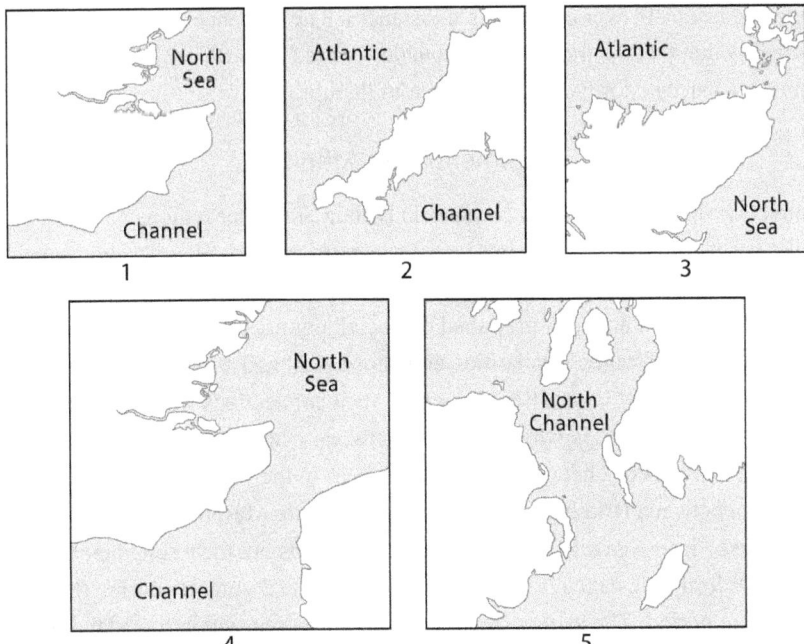

Figure 23 Details of three areas in which important seaways converged, and two regions in which narrow channels separated Britain from its neighbours

routes converged. Here members of different communities might have met, and new relations could develop from the encounter. In Britain there were three such places and all of them assumed a distinctive character. The earliest developments were in Orkney and the northern mainland of Scotland where local communities were able to control movement between the North Sea and the Atlantic, as they did in the Viking Age. It was here that some of the greatest Neolithic monuments were constructed. Another pivotal region was southwest England which included important sources of copper, gold, and tin. In the Early Bronze Age, rich burials illustrate the significance of this region, and during subsequent phases important sites were associated with the acquisition and working of metals. The same applied to Thanet where the Channel joined the North Sea. From the late third millennium BC the former island included a substantial number of round barrows (they were as densely distributed as those around Stonehenge), and in the earlier first millennium BC the same area contained an unparalleled concentration of middens, ringworks, metalworking sites, and hoards.

A second feature concerns coastal geography. Ireland is visible from part of Scotland, and France from southeast England. The narrow passages between them would have been easy to control (Earle et al. 2015). That was especially important during the Atlantic Bronze Age when boats carried ingots and finished artefacts over considerable distances. The evidence for armed conflict suggests that that the transport of valuables carried obvious dangers. Where the seaways narrowed it would be possible to disrupt it.

Alignments and Affinities

Direct comparisons between prehistoric Britain and other regions have always given problems and some claims have been extraordinary. How far did connections between Britain and its neighbours reach during the pre-Roman period, and what light, if any, can they shed on social identities? A basic distinction is between long-distance similarities and those confined to smaller areas. It is equally important to ask when and where such connections were rejected.

One starting point is where contacts between nearby communities seem to have been avoided. There are obvious instances in the study area: the restricted contacts between Britain and Ireland during the late Mesolithic phase, and the absence of Iron Age hillforts in one of these islands but their abundance in the other. A further instance is the lack of Cross-Channel contacts during the Late Neolithic period. The same process can be recognised within the island itself: the rarity of causewayed enclosures in the north where the first cursuses were built, and the restricted distribution of regular Bronze Age field systems.

Conversely, long-established kinds of monuments were still constructed in the north and west long after they had gone out of use in southern England. People elected to resist widespread developments as often as they followed them, and sometimes they adhered to traditional practices in the face of change. That could be why some of the largest henges and stone circles were erected *after* the new developments associated with Beakers and metalwork.

In other instances, relationships were established between the inhabitants of Britain and their immediate neighbours in Ireland and on the Continent. Sometimes they are documented by portable artefacts, principally ceramics and metalwork, but still stronger connections are evidenced by settlement patterns and monuments. An obvious instance is the distribution of co-axial fields which extended across the Channel and the southern North Sea. Another was the construction of ringworks during the early first millennium BC. Distinctive practices were also shared between the offshore island and the Continent: the idiosyncratic character of metalwork deposits – both hoards and river finds – during the Bronze Age, and the deposition of bodies in Iron Age storage pits. Not all the connections with the near-Continent extended far inland, and sometimes they were strongest towards the coast where communications were easier by sea. The most obvious examples include the distribution of precious cups along both sides of the Channel during the Early Bronze Age, the adoption of roundhouses of English type in northern France, and the defensive and domestic structures shared between the Iron Ages of western Britain and Atlantic Europe. Other features connected Britain with Ireland. The closest comparisons concern the architecture of Neolithic chambered tombs, the forms of the earliest metalwork, and the building of the first hillforts.

There were still longer alignments. They took two main forms. In some cases, they were based on a shared conception of the past, and in others they were characterised by long-distance networks connecting remote areas. Stonehenge and its surroundings illustrate both patterns. It was built amidst the remains of older monuments, including long barrows and causewayed enclosures whose forms seem to have referred to shared origins on the Continent. At the same time the sarsen structure was ringed by burials established after the first monoliths were erected. If its siting acknowledged the presence of older earthworks, these graves contained the bodies of people whose ancestors had settled in England after Stonehenge was built – they acknowledged the power of a past in which their forebears had no place. At the same time the burials with Beaker pottery were organised according to conventions shared with societies on the Continent. In this way they might have celebrated different affinities and origins.

The burial mounds around Stonehenge illustrate another observation. They included an exceptional variety of finely crafted grave goods, some which were made of non-local materials, including copper, bronze, gold, amber, and jet. Their characteristic forms were shared with artefacts in distant areas: Northwest France, Central Europe, and even the Aegean. Isotopic analysis shows that not all the people buried on Salisbury Plain had lived in the vicinity, but in death it seems to have been important to associate them with the power of this ancient monument. It was also necessary to emphasise their wider connections, extending across the Continent.

It is not the only evidence for a specialised network of this kind, and during other periods the close relationship between Britain and its immediate neighbours was crosscut by other long-distance alignments. The earliest was the distribution of jadeitite axes from the Alps, and in the Late Neolithic period another connection is illustrated by a style of rock art distributed from Iberia to northern Britain (Valdez-Tullett 2019). Early Bronze Age networks were almost as extensive, and during this phase communities in Wessex were related to those in Brittany and the Únětice Culture. The links with the Aegean might have been exceptional, but all these connections were significant. Even longer networks developed between 1300 and 800 BC when the interchange of artefacts and raw materials linked Britain to Spain in one direction and to Scandinavia in the other.

Finally, it is important to emphasise the local level. Just as Britain was drawn into a few long-distance networks, it was almost entirely excluded from others; the same was true of parts of the near-Continent. During most phases northern France, Belgium, north Germany, and the Low Countries did not participate in the main developments in prehistoric Europe. Although some regions shared a selection of high-quality artefacts, their Early Bronze Age settlements did not contain massive dwellings like those of the Únětice Culture. Those regions were beyond the distribution of Iron Age *Fürstensitze* with their links to the Mediterranean; and the rich burials that eventually took their place have surprisingly few close parallels in the study area. The same applies to the large Late Iron Age settlements known as *oppida*. When they first developed, the most complex examples were outside the region studied here. But they were established in Britain after Caesar's two expeditions.

As Kristiansen and Larsson observed, there were important distinctions between the complex archaeology of Scandinavia and Central Europe, and the simpler archaeological record of Britain and its immediate neighbours (Kristiansen & Larsson 2005: 210–2). It has been conventional to distinguish insular developments from those on the Continent. But another approach is to compare the results of fieldwork around the coasts of northern France and the Low Countries with the situation in regions further inland. Perhaps there was a difference between societies who were accustomed to travelling by sea and the

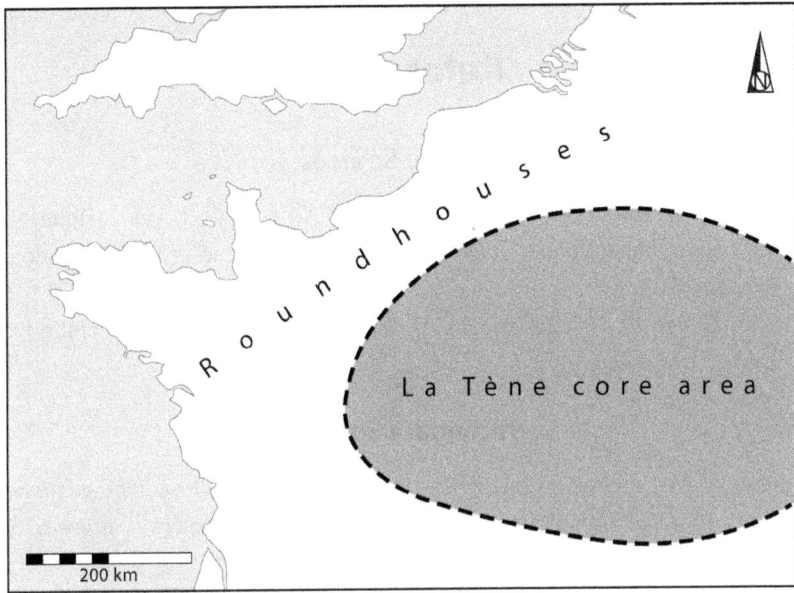

Figure 24 The La Tène core area in relation to the distribution of Bronze and Iron Age roundhouses close to the Channel coast

people who inhabited landlocked areas. In that case the differences on which most twentieth-century studies were based might have to be reconsidered. The parts of the Continent closest to Britain had a distinctive character because their inhabitants occupied an area in between two different worlds. They drew elements from their neighbours but retained distinctive properties of their own (Figure 24). This transcended the modern boundaries between countries separated by the sea.

Insularity and identity: how useful are these terms today? The physical separation between Britain and its neighbours was inescapable, but the desire to overcome that division changed over time and from one area to another as the people who lived on this island chose whether to ally themselves with other groups or to remain aloof. During different phases they took each of these courses. No doubt there were local connections and local variations, but on a larger scale the distinction between 'Britain' and 'Europe' meant very little in the prehistoric period. To distinguish between them today is an impediment to archaeological research.

References

Primary Sources

Gildas, *On the Ruin of Britain*. Translated by J. Giles 1841. London: Bohn.
Julius Caesar, *The Conquest of Gaul*. Translated by S. Handford 1982. London: Penguin.
Strabo, *Geography*. Translated by D. Roller 2020. Cambridge: Cambridge University Press.

Secondary Sources

Allentoft, M., Sikora, M., Fischer, A., et al. 2024. 100 ancient genomes show repeated population turnovers in Neolithic Denmark. *Nature* 625: 329–37.
Amkreutz L., & van der Vaart-Verschoof, S. 2022. *Doggerland: Lost World under the North Sea*. Leiden: Sidestone.
Arnoldussen, S., Johnston, R. & Løvschal, M. (eds.) 2021. *Europe's Early Fieldscapes*. Cham: Springer.
Atkinson, R. 1956. *Stonehenge*. Harmondsworth: Penguin.
Baczkowski, J. 2014. Learning by experience: The flint mines of southern England and their Continental origins. *Oxford Journal of Archaeology* 33: 135–53.
Ballin, T. B. 2016. Rising waters and processes of diversification and unification in material culture. *Journal of Quaternary Science* 32: 329–39.
Barrett, J., Bradley R., & Green, M. 1990. *Landscape, Monuments and Society: The Prehistory of Cranborne Chase*. Cambridge: Cambridge University Press.
Booth, T. 2019. A stranger in a strange land? A perspective on archaeological responses to the palaeogenetic revolution from an archaeologist working among palaeogeneticists. *World Archaeology* 51: 586–601.
Booth, T., Brück, J., Brace, S., & Barnes, I. 2021. Tales from the supplementary information: Ancestry change in Chalcolithic – Early Bronze Age Britain was gradual with varied kinship organisation. *Cambridge Archaeological Journal* 31: 379–400.
Bostyn, F., Lech, J., Saville, A., & Werra D. (eds.) 2023. *Prehistoric Flint Mines in Europe*. Oxford: Archaeopress.
Bourgeois Q. 2013. *Monuments on the Horizon: The Formation of the Barrow Landscape throughout the 3rd and 2nd Millennium BC*. Leiden: Sidestone.

Bourgeois Q. & Fontijn, D. 2008. Bronze Age houses and barrows in the Low Countries: an overview. In S. Arnoldussen & H. Fokkens (eds.), *Bronze Age Settlements in the Low Countries*. Oxford: Oxbow, pp. 41–57.

Bourgeois, J., & Talon, M. 2009. From Picardy to Flanders: Transmanche connection in the Bronze Age. In P. Clark (ed.), *Bronze Age Connections: Cultural Contact in Prehistoric Europe*. Oxford: Oxbow, pp. 38–59.

Brace, S., Dickmann, Y., Booth, T. et al. 2019. Ancient genomes indicate population replacement in Early Neolithic Britain. *Nature Ecology and Evolution* 3: 765–71.

Bradley, R. 2017. *A Geography of Offerings: Deposits of Valuables in the Landscapes of Ancient Europe*. Oxford: Oxbow.

Bradley, R. 2019 *The Prehistory of Britain and Ireland*. 2nd ed. Cambridge: Cambridge University Press.

Bradley, R. 2021. *Temporary Palaces: The Great House in European Prehistory*. Oxford: Oxbow.

Bradley, R. 2023a. *Monumental Times*. Oxford: Oxbow.

Bradley, R. 2023b. Long distance connections within Britain and Ireland: The evidence of insular rock art. *Proceedings of the Prehistoric Society* 89: 249–71.

Bradley, R. 2024. Beyond the bluestones: Links between distant monuments in Late Neolithic Britain and Ireland. *Antiquity* 98: 821–8.

Bradley, R., Entwistle, R., & Raymond, F. 1994. *Prehistoric Land Divisions on Salisbury Plain*. London: English Heritage.

Bradley, R., Haselgrove, C., Webley, L., & Vander Linden, M. 2016. *The Later Prehistory of Northwest Europe: The Evidence of Development-led Fieldwork*. Oxford: Oxford University Press.

Bradley, R., & Nimura, C. (eds.) 2016. *The Use and Reuse of Stone Circles*. Oxford: Oxbow.

Bradley, R., Rogers, A., Sturt, F., & Watson, A. 2016. Maritime havens in earlier prehistoric Britain. *Proceedings of the Prehistoric Society* 82: 125–59.

Bradley, R., & Watson, A. 2024. Sailing to Calanais: Monument complexes and the sea in the west of Scotland and beyond. *Proceedings of the Prehistoric Society* 90: 253–77.

Brindley, A., & Lanting, J. 1990. Radiocarbon dates for Neolithic single burials. *Journal of Irish Archaeology* 5: 1–7.

Brophy, K. 2016. *Reading between the Lines: The Neolithic Cursus Monuments of Scotland*. Abingdon: Routledge.

Brück, J. 2019. *Personifying Prehistory*. Oxford: Oxford University Press.

Brudnell, M., & Cooper, A. 2008. Post-middenism: Depositional histories on later Bronze Age settlements at Broom, Bedfordshire. *Oxford Journal of Archaeology* 27: 15–36.

Burgess, C., & Shennan, S. 1976. The Beaker phenomenon: Some suggestions. In C. Burgess & R. Miket (eds.), *Settlement and Economy in the Third and Second Millennia BC*. Oxford: British Archaeological Reports, pp. 309–31.

Burrow, S. 2010a. The formative henge: speculations drawn from the circular tradition of Wales and adjacent countries. . In J. Leary, T. Darvill, & D. Field (eds.), *Round Mounds and Monumentality in the British Neolithic and Beyond*. Oxford: Oxbow, pp. 182–96.

Burrow, S. 2010b. Bryn Celli Ddu: Alignment, construction, date and ritual. *Proceedings of the Prehistoric Society* 76: 249–70.

Card, N., Edmonds, M., & Mitchell, A. (eds.) 2020. *The Ness of Brodgar as it Stands*. Kirkwall: The Orcadian.

Carlin, N. 2017. Getting into the groove: Exploring the relationship between Grooved Ware and developed passage tombs in Ireland c. 3000–2700 cal BC. *Proceedings of the Prehistoric Society* 83: 155–88.

Case, H. 1993. Beakers: Deconstruction and after. *Proceedings of the Prehistoric Society* 59: 241–68.

Cassidy, L., Ó Maldúin, R., Kador, T. et al. 2020. A dynastic elite in monumental Neolithic society. *Nature* 582 (7812): 384–8.

Champion, T. 2013. Food technology and culture in the Late Bronze Age of southern Britain: perforated clay plates of the Lower Thames Valley. *Proceedings of the Prehistoric Society* 80: 279–98.

Champion, T. 2024. Iron and iron technology. In C. Haselgrove, K. Rebay-Salisbury & P. Wells (eds.), *The Oxford Handbook of the European Iron Age*. Oxford: Oxford University Press, pp. 773–96.

Childe, V. G. 1925. *The Dawn of European Civilisation*. London: Kegan, Paul, Trench.

Clark, J. D. G. 1966. The invasion hypothesis in British archaeology. *Antiquity* 40: 172–89.

Clarke, D. L. 1970. *Beaker Pottery of Great Britain and Ireland*. Cambridge: Cambridge University Press.

Cleal, R. 2012. Missing the point: Implications of the appearance and development of transverse arrowheads in southern Britain. In A. Meirion-Jones, J. Pollard, M. Allen, & J. Gardiner (eds.), *Image, Memory and Monumentality*. Oxford: The Prehistoric Society, pp. 136–45.

Cleal, R., Walker, K., & Montague, R. 1995. *Stonehenge in its Landscape: Twentieth Century Excavations*. London: English Heritage.

Cleary, R. 2015. Excavations at Grange Stone Circle B, Lough Gur, Co. Limerick, and a review of the dating. *Journal of Irish Archaeology* 24: 51–77.

Collis, J. 2003. *The Celts: Origins, Myths and Inventions*. Stroud.: Tempus.

Conneller, C. 2022. *Mesolithic Britain: Landscape and Society in Times of Change*. Abingdon: Routledge.

Cooper, A. 2016. 'Held in place': Round barrows in the later Bronze Age of lowland Britain. *Proceedings of the Prehistoric Society* 82: 291–322.

Copper, M., Whittle, A., & Sheridan, A. (eds.), 2024. *Revisiting Grooved Ware*. Oxford: Oxbow.

Cotter, C. 2012. *The Western Stone Forts Project*. Dublin: Wordwell.

Creighton, J. 2000. *Coins and Power in Late Iron Age Britain*. Cambridge: Cambridge University Press.

Cunliffe, B. 1987. *Hengistbury Head, Dorset, vol. 1*. Oxford: Oxford University Committee for Archaeology.

Cunliffe, B. 2001a. *The Extraordinary Voyage of Pytheas the Greek*. London: Allen Lane.

Cunliffe, B. 2001b. *Facing the Ocean: The Atlantic and Its Peoples*. Oxford: Oxford University Press.

Cunliffe, B. 2005. *Iron Age Communities in Britain*. 4th ed. Abingdon: Routledge.

Davis, O. 2013. Re-interpreting the Danebury assemblage: Houses, households and communities. *Proceedings of the Prehistoric Society* 79: 353–75.

Davis, S., & Rassmann, K. 2021. Beyond Newgrange: Brú na Bóinne in the later Neolithic. *Proceedings of the Prehistoric Society* 87: 189–218.

Delattre, V. 2000. De la relegation sociale à l'hypothèse des offrandes: l'exemple des depots en silos protohistoriques au confluent Seine-Yonne (Seine-et-Marne). *Révue archéologique du Centre de la France* 39: 5–30.

Delrieu, F. 2013. Chronologie et statut des sites fortifiés de hauteur au Bronze final et au premier Fer dans le Nord-Ouest de la France. In S. Krausz, A. Colin, K. Gruel, et al. (eds.), *L'Âge du fer en Europe*. Bordeaux: Maison de l'Archéologie, pp. 131–46.

Demoule, J. P. 1999. *Chronologie et société dans les nécropoles celtiques de la culture Aisne-Marne*. Revue Archéologique de Picardie, numéro special 15.

Earle, T., Ling, J., Uhnér, C. et al. 2015. The political economy and metal trade in Bronze Age Europe: understanding regional variability in terms of comparative advantage and articulations. *European Journal of Archaeology* 18: 633–57.

Edmonds, M. 2021. *Orcadia*. London: Head of Zeus.

Eogan, G. 1994. *The Accomplished Art: Gold and Gold-Working in Britain and Ireland during the Bronze Age*. Oxford: Oxbow.

Eogan, G., & Cleary, K. 2017. *The Passage Tomb Archaeology of the Great Mound at Knowth*. Dublin: Royal Irish Academy.

Evans, C. 2016. *Twice-crossed River*. Cambridge: Cambridge Archaeological Unit.

Farley, J., & Joy, J. 2024. *The Snettisham Hoards*. London: British Museum.

Fernández-Götz, M. 2019. A world of 200 oppida. In L. van Ligt and J. Bintliff (eds.), *Regional Systems in the Roman World, 150 BCE – 250 CE*. Leiden: Brill, pp. 35–66.

Fernández-Götz, M., & Ralston, I. 2017. The complexity and fragility of Early Iron Age urbanism in West-Central temperate Europe. *Journal of World Prehistory* 30: 259–79.

Fichtl, S. 2005. *Le ville celtique: les oppida de 150 av. J-C à 15 ap. J-C*. Paris: Errance.

Fitzpatrick, A. 2011. *The Amesbury Archer and the Boscombe Bowmen*. Salisbury: Wessex Archaeology.

Fitzpatrick, A., Haselgrove, C., & Lowther, P. 2013. Continuity and change at the end of the 2nd century BC in southern England and the cross-Channel zone. In V. Guichard (ed.), *Continuités et discontinuiés à la fin du IIe siècle avant notre ère*. Glux-en-Glenne: Bibracte, pp. 201–25.

Fontijn, D., & Fokkens, H. 2007. The emergence of early Iron Age 'chieftains' graves' in the southern Netherlands: Reconsidering transformations in burial and depositional practices. In C. Haselgrove & R. Pope (eds.), *The Earlier Iron Age in Britain and the Near Continent*. Oxford: Oxbow, pp. 354–73.

Fox, C. 1932. *The Personality of Britain: Cardiff*: National Museum of Wales.

Gardiner, J. 2008. On the production of discoidal knives and changing patterns of specialist flint production on the South Downs, England. *Analecta Praehistorica Leidensia* 40: 235–46.

Garrow, D. & Gosden, C. 2012. *Technologies of Enchantment: Exploring Celtic Art: 400 BC – AD 100*. Oxford: Oxford University Press.

Garrow, D., Gosden, C., Hill, J. D., & Bronk Ramsay, C. 2009. Dating Celtic Art: A major radiocarbon dating programme of Iron Age and early Roman metalwork in Britain. *Archaeological Journal* 166: 79–123.

Garwood, P. 2007. Before the hills in order stood: Chronology, time and history in the interpretation of early Bronze Age round barrows. In J. Last (ed.), *Beyond the Grave – New Perspectives on Barrows*. Oxford: Oxbow, pp. 30–52.

Gibson, A. 2005. *Stonehenge and Timber Circles*. 2nd ed. Stroud: Tempus.

Gibson, A. (ed.), 2019. *Bell Beaker Settlement of Europe*. Oxford: The Prehistoric Society.

Gibson, A., & Bayliss, A. 2009. Recent research at Duggleby Howe, North Yorkshire. *Archaeological Journal* 166: 39–78.

Gibson, C. 2016. Closed for business or cultural changes? Tracing the reuse and final blocking of megalithic tombs during the Beaker period. In J. Koch & B. Cunliffe (ed.), *Celtic from the West 3*. Oxford: Oxbow, pp. 83–110.

Giles, M. 2012. *A Forged Glamour: Landscape, Identity and Material Culture in the Iron Age*. Oxford: Windgather Press.

Gosden, C., Green, C., Cooper, A., et al. 2021. *English Landscapes and Identities*. Oxford: Oxford University Press.

Greaney, S., Hazell, Z., Barclay, A., et al. 2020. Tempo of a mega-henge: A new chronology for Mount Pleasant, Dorchester, Dorset. *Proceedings of the Prehistoric Society* 86: 199–236.

Griffiths, C. 2023. Axes to axes: The chronology, distribution and composition of recent Bronze Age hoards from Britain and Northern Ireland. *Proceedings of the Prehistoric Society* 89: 179–205.

Griffiths, S. 2014. Points in time: The Mesolithic-Neolithic transition and the chronology of late rod microliths in Britain. *Oxford Journal of Archaeology* 33: 221–43.

Griffiths, S., Carlin, N., Thomas, J., et al. 2023. Events, narratives and data. *Journal of Social Archaeology* 23: 183–92.

Gron, K., & Sørensen, L. 2018. Cultural and economic negotiation: a new perspective on the Neolithic transition of southern Scandinavia. *Antiquity* 92: 958–74.

Hamilton, D., Haselgrove, C., & Gosden C. 2015. The impact of Bayesian chronologies on the British Iron Age. *World Archaeology* 24: 642–60.

Haughton, M., & Løvschal, M. 2023. Ancestral commons: the deep-time emergence of Bronze Age pastoral mobility. *Antiquity* 97: 1470–87.

Hawkes, C. 1940. *The Prehistoric Foundations of Europe to the Mycenaean Age*. London: Methuen.

Helms, M. 2012, Nourishing a structured world with living metal in Bronze Age Europe. *World Art* 2: 105–18.

Henderson, J. 2007. *The Atlantic Iron Age: Settlement and Identity in the First Millennium BC*. London: Routledge.

Hingley, R. 2022. *Conquering the Ocean: The Roman Invasion of Britain*. Oxford: Oxford University Press.

Hofmann, D., Frieman, C., Furholt, M., et al. 2024. *Negotiating Migrations: The Archaeology and Politics of Mobility*. London: Bloomsbury.

Jacobi, R. 1976. Britain inside and outside Mesolithic Europe. *Proceedings of the Prehistoric Society* 42: 67–84.

Johnston, R. 2021. *Bronze Age Worlds: A Social Prehistory of Britain and Ireland*. Abingdon: Routledge.

Jope, E. M. 2000. *Celtic Art in the British Isles*. Oxford: Clarendon Press.

Kaesar, M.-A. 2022. *La Tène: A Place of Memory*. Hauterive: Latènium.

Knight, M., Ballantyne, R., Brudnell, M. et al. 2024. *Must Farm Pile-dwelling Settlement*. Cambridge: McDonald Institute for Archaeological Research.

Knight, M. G. 2021. *Fragments of the Bronze Age: The Destruction and Deposition of Metalwork in South-West Britain and its Wider Context*. Oxford: Oxbow.

Krausz, S. 2019. Iron Age fortifications on France. In G. Lock & I. Ralston (eds.), *Hillforts: Britain, Ireland and the Nearer Continent*, 165–87. Oxford: Archaeopress.

Kristiansen, K. 2022. *Archaeology and the Genetic Revolution in European Prehistory*. Cambridge: Cambridge University Press.

Kristiansen, K., & Larsson, T. 2005. *The Rise of Bronze Age Society: Travels, Transmissions and Transformations*. Cambridge: Cambridge University Press.

Lamb, A. 2022. Iron Age mortuary practices in Britain: An account of current trends and their characteristics within contemporary northwestern European traditions. *Proceedings of the Prehistoric Society* 88: 227–60.

Laporte, L. & Tinévez, J.-Y. 2005. Neolithic houses and chambered tombs of western France. *Cambridge Archaeological Journal* 14: 217–34.

Lawrence, T., Donnelly, M., Kennard, L. et al. 2023. Britain in or out of Europe during the late Mesolithic? A new perspective on the Mesolithic – Neolithic transition. *Open Archaeology* 8(1): 550–77.

Leary, J., Field, D., & Campbell, G. (eds.) 2013. *Silbury Hill*. Swindon: English Heritage.

Le Bihan, J.-P. & Villard, J.-F. 2010. *Archéologie d'une île à la pointe d'Europe*. Rennes: SRA Bretagne.

Lehoërff, A. 2012. *Par-delà l'horizon. Sociétés en Manche et mer du Nord, il y a 3500 ans*. Paris: Somogy éditions d'art.

Lehoërff, A., & Talon, M. (eds.) 2017. *Movement, Exchange and Identity in Europe in the 1st and 2nd Millennia BC: Beyond Frontiers*. Oxford: Oxbow.

Ling, J., Díaz-Guardamino, M., Horn, C. et al. 2024. *Bronze Age Rock Art in Iberia and Scandinavia. Words, Warriors and the Long-distance Metal Trade*. Oxford: Oxbow.

Ling, J., Earle, T., & Kristiansen, K. 2018. Maritime mode of production: Raiding and trading in seafaring chiefdoms. *Current Anthropology* 59: 488–524.

Lock, G., & Ralston, I. 2022. *Atlas of Hillforts in Britain and Ireland*. Edinburgh: Edinburgh University Press.

Løvschal, M. 2014. Emerging boundaries: Social embedment of landscape and settlement divisions in northwestern Europe during the first millennium BC. *Current Anthropology* 55: 725–50.

Madgwick, R., Lamb, A., Sloane, S., et al. 2019. Multi-isotope analysis reveals that feasts in the Stonehenge environs and across Wessex drew people and animals throughout Britain. *Science Advances* 5(3).

Manby, T., King, A., & Vyner, B. 2003. The Neolithic and Early Bronze Age: a time of early agriculture. In T. Manby, S. Moorhouse, & P. Ottaway (eds.), *The Archaeology of Yorkshire*. Leeds: Yorkshire Archaeological Society, pp. 35–116.

Mare, E., Ghesquière, E., Le Goff, I. et al. 2018. Malleville-sur-le-Bec. Un village de l'âge du Bronze final. In S. Boulud-Gazo & M. Mélin (eds.), *Contributions à l'archéologie de l'âge du Bronze dans les espaces atlantiques et Manche-Mer du Nord*. Poiré-sur-Vie: Association des recherches sur l'âge du Bronze, pp. 77–278.

McClatchie, M., Barratt, P., & Bogaard, A. 2016. The changing face of Neolithic and Bronze Age Ireland: A big data approach to the settlement and burial record. *Journal of World Prehistory* 29: 117–53.

McKinley, J., Leivers, M., Schuster, J., et al. 2014. *Cliffs End Farm, Isle of Thanet*, Kent. Salisbury: Wessex Archaeology.

McOmish, D. 2020. Characterising 'communities' in the Early Iron Age of southern Britain. In B. Currás & I. Sastre (eds.), *Alternative Iron Ages*. Abingdon: Routledge, pp. 3–30.

Milcent, P.-Y. 2006. Premier âge de Fer médio-atlantique et genèse multipolaire de cultures matérielles latènnes. In D. Vitali (ed.), *Celtes et Gaules*. Glux-en-Glenne: Bibracte, pp. 81–105.

Milcent, P.-Y. 2012. *Au temps des elites en Gaule atlantique*. Rennes: Presses Universitaires de Rennes.

Mithen, S. 2022. How long was the Mesolithic-Neolithic overlap in western Scotland? Evidence from the 4th millennium BC on the Isle of Islay and the evaluation of three scenarios for Mesolithic-Neolithic interaction. *Proceedings of the Prehistoric Society* 88: 53–77.

Montelius, O. 1908. The chronology of the British Bronze Age. *Archaeologia* 61: 97–162.

Moore, T., & Armada, X.-L. (eds.) 2011. *Atlantic Europe in the First Millennium BC*. Oxford: Oxford University Press.

Nash, D., Oborowski, J., Ullyott, J., et al. 2020. Origins of the sarsen megaliths at Stonehenge. *Science Advances* 6.

Needham, S. 1991. *Excavation and Salvage at Runnymede Bridge 1978: The Late Bronze Age Waterfront Site*. London: British Museum Press.

Needham, S. 2000 Power pulses across a cultural divide: Cosmologically driven acquisition between Armorica and Wessex. *Proceedings of the Prehistoric Society* 66: 151–207.

Needham, S. 2005. Transforming Beaker culture in North West Europe: Processes of fission and fusion. *Proceedings of the Prehistoric Society* 71: 171–217.

Needham, S. 2007. 800 BC. The great divide. In C. Haselgrove & R. Pope (eds.), *The Earlier Iron Age in Britain and the Near Continent*. Oxford: Oxbow, pp. 39–63.

Needham, S. 2009. Encompassing the sea: 'Maritories' and Bronze Age maritime interactions. In P. Clark (ed.), *Bronze Age Connections: Cultural Contact in Prehistoric Europe*. Oxford: Oxbow, pp. 12–37.

Needham, S. 2012. Case and place for the British Chalcolithic. In M. Allen, J. Gardiner, & A. Sheridan (eds.), *Is there a British Chalcolithic?* Oxford: The Prehistoric Society, pp. 1–26.

Needham, S. 2024. From barrowscape to fieldscape. In P. Doyle (ed.), *Boyne and Beyond*. Dublin: Wordwell, pp. 74–87.

Needham, S., & Bowman, S. 2005. Flesh-hooks. Technological complexity and the Atlantic Bronze Age feasting complex. *European Journal of Archaeology* 8(2): 93–136.

Needham, S., Parfitt, K., & Varndell, G. 2006. *The Ringlemere Cup: Precious Cups and the Beginning of the Channel Bronze Age*. London: British Museum.

Needham, S., & Wilkin, N. 2024. British ceremonial weapons revisited. In L. Amkreutz & D. Fontijn (eds.), *Larger than Life*. Leiden: Sidestone, pp. 235–69.

O'Brien, W. 2004. *Ross Island. Mining, Metal and Society in Early Ireland*. Galway: Department of Archaeology, National University of Ireland, Galway.

O'Brien, W. 2015. *Prehistoric Copper Mining in Europe 5500 – 500 BC*. Oxford: Oxford University Press.

O'Brien, W., & O'Driscoll, J. 2017. *Hillforts, Warfare and Society in Bronze Age Ireland*. Oxford: Archaeopress.

O'Connor, B. 2010. From Dorchester to Dieskau – some aspects of relations between Britain and Central Europe during the Early Bronze Age. In H. Meller & F. Bertemes (eds.), *Der Griff nach den Sternen*. Halle: Tagungen des Landesmuseums für Vorgeschichte Halle, pp. 591–602.

O'Driscoll, J. 2024. Exploring the Baltinglass cursus complex: Routes for the dead. *Antiquity* 98: 636–53.

Olalde, I., Brace, S., Allentoft, M., et al. 2018. The Beaker phenomenon and the genomic transformation of northwest Europe. *Nature* 555: 190–6.

O'Kelly, C., Cleary, R., & Lehane, D. 1983. *Newgrange Co. Meath, Ireland: The Late Neolithic / Beaker Period Settlement*. Oxford: British Archaeological Reports.

O'Sullivan, M., Davis, S., & Stout, G. 2012. Henges in Ireland: new discoveries and emerging issues. In A. Gibson (ed.), *Enclosing the Neolithic*. Oxford: British Archaeological Reports, pp. 37–53.

Oswald, A., Dyer, C., & Barber, M. 2001. *The Creation of Monuments: Neolithic Causewayed Enclosures in the British Isles*. Swindon: English Heritage.

Outram, A., & Bogaard, A. 2019. *Subsistence and Society in Prehistory*. Cambridge: Cambridge University Press.

Pare, C. 2000. Bronze and the Bronze Age. In C. Pare (ed.), *Metals Make the World Go Round: The Supply and Circulation of Metals in Bronze Age Europe*. Oxford: Oxbow, pp. 1–38.

Parker Pearson, M. 2023. *Stonehenge: A Brief History*. London: Bloomsbury Academic.

Parker Pearson, M., Sheridan, A., Jay, M., et al. 2019. *The Beaker People. Isotopes, Mobility and Diet in Prehistoric Britain*. Oxford: The Prehistoric Society.

Parker Pearson, M., Pollard, J., Richards, C. et al. 2020. *Stonehenge for the Ancestors: Part 1*. Leiden: Sidestone.

Parker Pearson, M., Bevins, R., Bradley, R. et al. 2024. Stonehenge and its Altar Stone: the significance of distant stone sources. *Archaeology International* 27: 113–37.

Patterson, N., Isakov, M., Booth, T., et al. 2022. Large-scale migration into Britain during the Middle to Late Bronze Age. *Nature* 601: 588–94.

Peake, R. 2020. *Villiers-sun-Seine: un habitat aristocratique de IXe siècle avant notre ère*. Paris: CNRS Éditions.

Pétrequin, P., Cassen, S., Errera, M., et al. 2012. *Jade: Grandes haches alpines du Néolithique européen*. Besançon: Presses Universitaires de Franche-Comté.

Pioffet, H. 2015. *Sociétés et identités de premier Néolithique de Grand-Bretagne at d'Irlande dans leur context nord européen*. Rennes: Université de Rennes.

Pope, R. 2015. Bronze Age architectural traditions: dates and landscapes. In F. Hunter & I. Ralston (eds.), *Scotland in Later Prehistoric Europe*. Edinburgh: Society of Antiquaries of Scotland, pp. 159–84.

Pope, R. 2022. Re-approaching Celts: Origins, society and social change. *Journal of Archaeological Research* 30: 1–67.

Raftery, B. 1984. *La Tène in Ireland: Problems of Origins and Chronology*. Marburg: Vorgeschichtlichen Seminar Marburg.

Rassmann, C. 2011. Identities overseas? The long barrows in Britain and Denmark. In M. Furholt, F. Lüth, & J. Müller (eds.), *Megaliths and Identities*. Bonn: Habelt, pp. 167–76.

Renfrew, C. 1973. Monuments, mobilisation and social organisation in Neolithic Wessex. In Renfrew, C. (ed.), *The Explanation of Culture Change*. London: Duckworth, pp. 539–58.

Richards, C. (ed.) 2013. *Building the Great Stone Circles of the North*. Oxford: Windgather.

Richards, C. & Jones, R. 2016. *The Development of Neolithic House Societies in Orkney*. Oxford: Windgather Press.

Riquier, V., Maitay, C., Leroi-Langelin, E., & Maguer, P. 2018 Maisons et dépendances à l'âge du Fer dans le nord et l'ouest de la France: du premier âge du Fer au début de La Tène. In A. Villard-Le Tiec (ed.), *Architectures de l'âge du Fer en Europe occidentale et centrale*. Rennes: Presses universitaires de Rennes, pp. 273–302.

Risch, R., Friederich, S., Küssner, M., & Meller, H. 2022. Architecture and settlement dynamics in Central Germany from the Late Neolithic to the Early Bronze Age. *Proceedings of the Prehistoric Society* 88: 123–54.

Risch, R., & Meller, H. 2015. Change and continuity in Europe and the Mediterranean around 1600 BC. *Proceedings of the Prehistoric Society* 81: 239–64.

Roberts, B., Boughton, D., Dinwiddy, D., et al. 2015. Collapsing commodities or lavish offerings? Understanding massive metalwork deposition at Langton Maltravers, Dorset, during the Bronze Age – Iron Age transition. *Oxford Journal of Archaeology* 34: 365–95.

Robin, G. 2009. *L'architecture des signes*. Rennes: Presses Universitaires de Rennes.

Ruiz-Gálvez Priego, M. 1998. *La Europa atlántica en la Edad del Bronce*. Barcelona: Crítica.

Scarre, C. 2011. *Landscapes of Neolithic Brittany*. Oxford: Oxford University Press.

Schier, W. (ed.) 2023. *Rondels Revisited: Recent Research on Neolithic Circular Enclosures in Central Europe*. Rahden: Marie Leidorf.

Schulz Paulsson, B. 2017. *Time and Stone: The Emergence and Development of Megaliths and Megalithic Societies in Europe*. Oxford: Archaeopress.

Schumann, R., & van der Vaart-Verschoof, S (eds.) 2017. *Perspectives on Contacts, Relations and Differentiation during the Early Iron Age Hallstatt C Period in Northwest and Central Europe*. Leiden: Sidestone.

Sharples, N. 2010. *Social Relations in Later Prehistory: Wessex in the First Millennium BC*. Oxford: Oxford University Press.

Sharples, N. 2014. Are the developed hillforts of southern England urban? In M. Fernández-Götz, H. Wendling, & K. Winger (eds.), *Paths to Complexity: Centralisation and Urbanisation in Iron Age Europe*. Oxford: Oxbow, pp. 224–32.

Shennan, S. 2013. Demographic continuities and discontinuities in Neolithic Europe: Evidence, methods and implications. *Journal of Archaeological Method and Theory* 20: 300–11.

Sheridan, A. 2013. Early Neolithic habitation structures in Britain and Ireland: a matter of circumstance and context. In D. Hofmann & J. Smyth (eds.), *Tracking the Neolithic House in Europe*. New York: Springer, pp. 283–300.

Sheridan, A., & Pétrequin, P. 2014. Constructing a narrative for the Neolithic of Britain and Ireland. *Proceedings of the British Academy* 198: 369–90.

Sims-Williams, P. 2020. An alternative to 'Celtic from the East' and 'Celtic from the West'. *Cambridge Archaeological Journal* 30: 511–29.

Sørensen, M. L. S., & Rebay-Salisbury, K. 2023. *Death and the Body in Bronze Age Europe*. Cambridge: Cambridge University Press.

Spazier, A., & Bertemes, F. 2018. The ring sanctuary of Pömmelte, Germany: A monumental multi-layer metaphor of the late third millennium BC. *Antiquity* 93: 655–73.

Standish, C., Dhuime, B., Hawkesworth, G., & Pike, A. 2015. A non-local source of Irish Chalcolithic and Early Bronze Age gold. *Proceedings of the Prehistoric Society* 81: 149–77.

Stevens, C., & Fuller, D. 2012. Did Neolithic farming fail? The case for a Bronze Age agricultural revolution in the British Isles. *Antiquity* 86: 707–22.

Stockhammer, P., & Massy, K. 2022. Mobility at the outset of the Bronze Age. In M. Fernández-Götz, C. Nimura, P. Stockhammer, & R. Cartwright (eds.), *Rethinking Migrations in Late Prehistoric Eurasia*. Oxford: Oxford University Press, pp. 170–88.

Thomas, J. 2010. The village people? Origin and development of 'aggregated' settlement in the East Midlands. In M. Sterry, A. Tullett, & N. Roy (eds.), *In Search of the Iron Age*. Leicester: Leicester University School of Archaeology and Ancient History, pp. 1–26.

Thomas, J. S. 2013. *The Birth of Neolithic Britain*. Oxford: Oxford University Press.

Timberlake, S. 2016. New ideas on the exploitation of copper, tin, gold and lead in Bronze Age Britain: The mining, smelting and movement of metal. *Materials and Manufacturing Processes* 32: 709–27.

Valdez-Tullett, J. 2019. *Design and Connectivity: The Case of Atlantic Rock Art*. Oxford: British Archaeological Reports.

Van de Noort, R. 2011. *North Sea Archaeologies*. Oxford: Oxford University Press.

Vander Linden, M. 2024. *The Beaker Phenomenon in Europe*. Cambridge: Cambridge University Press.

Vandkilde, H. 2017. *The Metal Hoard from Pile, Scania, Sweden*. Aarhus: Aarhus University Press.

Vannier, E. 2020. The funerary architecture of the La Tène period in north-western Gaul and southern Britain. *Proceedings of the Prehistoric Society* 86: 285–304.

Waddington, K., Bayliss, A., Higham, T., et al. 2019. Histories of deposition: Creating chronologies for the Late Bronze Age – Early Iron Age transition in southern Britain. *Archaeological Journal* 176: 84–133.

Webley, L. 2015. Rethinking Iron Age connections across the Channel and the North Sea. In H. Anderson-Whymark, D. Garrow, & F. Sturt (eds.), *Continental Connections: Exploring Cross-Channel Relationships from the Mesolithic to the Iron Age*. Oxford: Oxbow, pp. 122–44.

Whitehouse, N., Schulting, R., McClatchie, M., et al. 2014. Neolithic agriculture on the European western frontier: The boom and bust of early farming in Ireland. *Journal of Archaeological Science* 51: 181–205.

Whittle, A. 2020. The long and short of it: Memory and practice in the Early Neolithic of Britain and Ireland. In A. Barclay, D. Field, & J. Leary (eds.), *Houses of the Dead?* Oxford: Oxbow, pp. 79–90.

Whittle, A. 2023. Time re-gathered. In P. Lefranc, C. Croutsch, & A. Demaire (eds.), *Les enceintes Néolithiques du nord-ouest de 'Europe*. Dijon: Éditions universitaires de Dijon, pp. 385–401.

Whittle, A., Healy, F. & Bayliss, A., 2011. *Gathering Time: Dating the Early Neolithic Enclosures of Southern Britain and Ireland*. Oxford: Oxbow Books.

Whittle, A., Pollard. J., & Greaney, S. (eds.) 2023. *Ancient DNA and the Neolithic*. Oxford: Oxbow.

Wilkes, E., Pitman, D., Randall, C., & Brown, A. 2021. Think local, act global: Multi-scalar connections of Iron Age communities in Poole Harbour, Dorset, England. *Archaeological Journal* 178: 32–52.

Williams, A. 2023. *Boom and Bust in Bronze Age Britain: the Great Orme Copper Mine and European Trade*. Oxford: Archaeopress.

Williams, M. 2003. Growing metaphors: The agricultural cycle as metaphor in the later pre- historic period of Britain and North-Western Europe. *Journal of Social Archaeology* 3: 223–55.

Willis, C. 2021. *Stonehenge and Middle to Late Neolithic Cremation in Mainland Britain (c. 3500–2500 BC)*. Oxford: British Archaeological Reports.

Woodbridge, J., Fyfe, R., Roberts, N., et al. 2014. The impact of the Neolithic agricultural transition in Britain. A comparison of pollen-based land-cover and archaeological C 14 date-inferred population change. *Journal of Archaeological Science* 51: 2216–24.

Woodman, P. 2015. *Ireland's First Settlers. Time and the Mesolithic*. Oxford: Oxbow.

Woodward, A., & Hunter, J. 2015. *Ritual in Early Bronze Age Grave Goods*. Oxford: Oxbow.

Yates, D. 2007. *Land, Power and Prestige: Bronze Age Field Systems in Southern England*. Oxford: Oxbow.

York, J. 2002. The life cycle of Bronze Age metalwork from the Thames. *Oxford Journal of Archaeology* 21: 77–92.

Acknowledgements

I must thank Bettina Arnold and Manuel Fernández-Götz for their positive response to my proposal, and Aaron Watson for producing the illustrations to his usual high standard. Anwen Cooper kindly helped me with digital problems.

It is dedicated to my Reading colleague Amanda Clarke with whom I excavated in Scotland for many years. I offer it as a gift on her retirement from university teaching.

Cambridge Elements

The Archaeology of Europe

Manuel Fernández-Götz
University of Oxford

Manuel Fernández-Götz is Professor of Later European Prehistory at the University of Oxford. His research focuses on Iron Age and Roman societies in Europe, with a particular interest in questions of social identities, early urbanisation, and conflict archaeology. He has directed fieldwork projects in Spain, Germany, the United Kingdom, and Croatia.

Bettina Arnold
University of Wisconsin–Milwaukee

Bettina Arnold is a Full Professor of Anthropology at the University of Wisconsin–Milwaukee and Adjunct Curator of European Archaeology at the Milwaukee Public Museum. Her research interests include the archaeology of alcohol, the archaeology of gender, mortuary archaeology, Iron Age Europe, and the history of archaeology.

About the Series

Elements in the Archaeology of Europe is a collaborative publishing venture between Cambridge University Press and the European Association of Archaeologists. Composed of concise, authoritative, and peer-reviewed studies by leading scholars, each volume in this series will provide timely, accurate, and accessible information about the latest research into the archaeology of Europe from the Paleolithic era onwards, as well as on heritage preservation.

Cambridge Elements ≡

The Archaeology of Europe

Elements in the Series

A Comparative Study of Rock Art in Later Prehistoric Europe
Richard Bradley

Digital Innovations in European Archaeology
Kevin Garstki

Migration Myths and the End of the Bronze Age in the Eastern Mediterranean
A. Bernard Knapp

Salt: White Gold in Early Europe
Anthony Harding

Archaeology and the Genetic Revolution in European Prehistory
Kristian Kristiansen

Megasites in Prehistoric Europe: Where Strangers and Kinsfolk Met
Bisserka Gaydarska and John Chapman

The Bell Beaker Phenomenon in Europe
Marc Vander Linden

Archaeology of the Roman Conquest: Tracing the Legions, Reclaiming the Conquered
Manuel Fernández-Götz and Nico Roymans

Insularity and Identity: Prehistoric Britain and the Archaeology of Europe
Richard Bradley

A full series listing is available at: www.cambridge.org/EAE

For EU product safety concerns, contact us at Calle de José Abascal, 56–1°, 28003 Madrid, Spain or eugpsr@cambridge.org.

www.ingramcontent.com/pod-product-compliance
Lightning Source LLC
Chambersburg PA
CBHW060548210525
27036CB00014B/583